T0329052

FAMOUS – BUT NO CHILDREN

FAMOUS – BUT NO CHILDREN

J O RABER

Algora Publishing
New York

Library of Congress Cataloging-in-Publication Data —

Raber, J. O.
    Famous, but no children / J.O. Raber.
        pages cm
    Includes bibliographical references.
        ISBN 978-1-62894-042-8 (soft cover: alk. paper) — ISBN 978-1-62894-043-
5 (hard cover: alk. paper) — ISBN 978-1-62894-044-2 (e) 1. Childfree choice. 2.
Men. 3. Women. I. Title.
    HQ734.R117 2014
    306.87—dc23
                                2014001045

Printed in the United States

TABLE OF CONTENTS

INTRODUCTION

Why write a book about famous people who did not have children? First, this book is not anti-children; though it is about the travesty of children being born to irresponsible parents, and the negative impact irresponsible parenthood has had on the world. It is also about people who have made an important difference because they were more oriented toward making that difference than toward living the conventional life of rearing children. This is not to say that people with children have never made a difference; however, the accomplishments of many of history's great men and women were often the consequence of their non-conventionality and their non-procreation.

And true greatness should not be confused with fame. Every generation has its famous individuals, but relatively few of these famous folks make an indelible difference, though fame is much broader today than in past eras predating mass media. Radio, television, motion pictures and the internet can give contemporary celebrities instant national or even international recognition; however, many people blessed with fame and fortune have pursued hedonistic lifestyles with no higher social consciousness than the rest of humanity. Fame and fortune should carry with it the responsibility of uplifting the human spirit.

Also, for nearly every contemporary celebrity, there are many other individuals who might do as well if given the chance. Contemporary celebrities, more often than not, are annuals that quickly fade after their season in the sun; and then the sun shines on a new field of celebrities. The overwhelming majority of men and women included in this work are perennials. Nor did all of these 'perennials' gain fame as we know it today. Just as fame is not always accompanied by true greatness, true greatness is not always accompanied by fame.

As an example: Harriet Tubman was an escaped slave who helped hundreds of others find their way to freedom via the underground railroad, as it became known. Hers is not a name that most folks recognize, but her deeds certainly deserve recognition. Each time she brought people across to freedom, she put her own life on the line. Harriet had no children. Would she have put her own life repeatedly in harm's way if she had had children to rear? Would you?

Nellie Bly is another remarkable woman whose name is probably not on the tip of everyone's tongue today. Yet she virtually invented undercover investigative reporting, going undercover as an inmate in an insane asylum to expose atrocities there. Her courage was boundless. And she was always up to a challenge. She circumvented the globe in some seventy-two days and six hours. Until then, *Around the World in 80 Days* was only a fiction. Motherhood would have rendered such an exciting career nearly impossible. And she opened the doors for women reporters, who up 'til then just did fashion news and domestic columns.

Nor are the names of Maria Gaetana d'Agnesi and Maria Teresa d'Agnesi likely to come to mind in naming women of accomplishment. The former was a brilliant mathematician of significant importance in her day. She authored the book, *Analytical Institutions*, which was well received: most remarkable coming from a woman of her time. Her sister, Maria Teresa d'Agnesi, was a composer, librettist, harpsichordist and singer. They lived out their lives in eighteenth century Milan, Italy, and never had children.

Does the name William Tutte ring a bell? Probably not, but he was a British mathematician and cryptographer who helped crack the German code in World War II. He did not have children, nor did Hermann Gmeiner, who, following World War II, founded the *SOS Children's Villages* for war orphans. This developed into an international organization for placing orphaned and abandoned children in 'villages' with eight to ten children to a house; and to each house was assigned a foster mother. Gmeiner asked these foster mothers not to marry lest their commitment become divided. In turn, he remained unmarried.[1]

Relatively few names are 'household names' that everyone has heard of, but a far greater number of people are well-known and important within their respective spheres. For instance, how many of the world's great philosophers or physicists can you name? And if your interest is opera, you might not be able to rattle off the names of many major league baseball players; but if your interest is baseball, you might not be able to name that many celebrated opera singers. And how many singers can name the man who invented the microphone? He had no children, nor did the inventors of the cable car, the Ferris wheel, or the popular Scrabble game. Chances are, you've used one or more of these inventions but without knowing anything of their inventors. Thus, fame has its degrees.

This work includes lists of hundreds of history's famous child-free folks, at least famous within their respective professions. As you move your eyes through these names of men and women who did not sire or bear children, take time to notice the diversity represented here: the vast number of professions, the incredible accomplishments, the daring achievements, the marks these men and women left on history. While it is certainly the case that many of the world's great achievers had children, what is truly noteworthy is how many of them did not.

---

1 *Time Magazine*, Dec. 29, 1975, p.7, Saints Among Us: The Work of Mother Teresa, http://www.time.com/time/magazine/article/0,9171,945463-7,00.html

This book is not intended to 'flame' parents, but to examine some of the philosophical arguments that have been put forth on the child-free issue. Considering the impact of population growth from both environmental and sociological perspectives, this work advances the child-free philosophy as not only a moral life-style choice, but one that is becoming more and more prudent as the world population continues to inflate.

Author's note

For our purposes, the terms *'childless'* and *'child-free'* are defined as follows: *Childless* refers to people who would like to have children but don't have children for any one of a number of reasons: infertility, failure to find a suitable partner, economic hardship, etc. *Child-free* refers to people who don't want children for any one of a number of reasons: the world has too many problems, the world has too many people, career comes first, dedication to other interests in life, love of freedom, or simply no desire to have children. Child-free folks do not want children, now or later. Often, they have known since they themselves were children that they would never want to procreate. Many child-free folks had comfortable childhoods themselves, and were not abused or deprived as children.

Please keep in mind that since it's not always possible to know whether historic figures were childless or child-free, the term 'child-free' is sometimes used in this work where "childless' would be the correct terminology.

It is important to distinguish between childless and child-free because childless implies a lack of something whereas child-free implies freedom from something: freedom from procreation, freedom to live one's own life instead of trying to relive it through one's children, enslaving one's self and one's offspring in the process.

People have different interests, different paths to follow — or to lead.

CHAPTER 1. TO BEAR OR NOT TO BEAR: THAT IS THE QUESTION

There are those who have children and regret it; and there are those who don't have children and regret it. But it is far better to err on the side of not having children. If you regret having them, there is little you can do about it. If you regret not having them, there is plenty you can do. If it's too late to have your own, you can adopt or become a foster parent or godparent. If you have a special talent, mentor a child or group of children. Many parents want children who will follow in their footsteps, but their progeny often have other footsteps to follow. If you are childless/child-free you can mentor someone who shares similar aspirations as yourself. A biological connection is no guarantee of this. Or if the genetic connection is important to you, you can help raise nieces, nephews or young cousins. Everyone has an extended family. Get to know yours.

And remember, in a relationship in which one partner wants children and the other does not, this is the one issue where there is no room for compromise. Never pretend you do if you don't, or vice versa.

For those of you who believe that having children is a natural part of the life process, if I point out to you that Mother Teresa did not have children, and presumably by her own choice, you might respond with something like, "Of course not; she was a nun." And such an answer would suggest that you believe it's all right to be non child-bearing (or non child-siring) under certain circumstances. Then I would ask you to define those circumstances and explain how you arrived at your answer; and you might be at a loss for words.

One does not have to be a nun or a pope in order to have the right to forgo bearing or siring children. Many of the world's great artists, writers, scientists and reformers chose to forgo bearing or siring offspring. And it is likely that many of these geniuses and intellectuals would not have bestowed upon the world their gifts if they had been encumbered by child-rearing. Many young people have creative aspirations that fall by the wayside once they are locked into the child-rearing mode.

It is also worth mentioning here how relatively few women throughout history have achieved the status of great artists, writers, scientists and reformers, as compared with the number of men. Contrary to what generations of men wanted to believe, it was not for lack of talent or intelligence that women were historically denied such status. This gender oppression was owed in part to their role as mothers. Husbands had careers, while wives were expected to stay home and have babies. This was nothing less than class oppression; women were regarded as second class citizens at best. Of the relatively few women prior to the mid-20th century who did make history through their achievements, they were often women without children. For example:

> Jane Addams: Social reformer and first American woman
> awarded the Nobel Peace Prize
> Maria Gaetana d'Agnesi and Maria Teresa d'Agnesi: mentioned in the Introduction to this book
> Louisa May Alcott: Author of *Little Women* and other books[1]
> Marian Anderson: Afro-American opera singer
> Susan B. Anthony: Abolitionist and suffragist

---

1 Louisa May Alcott did not have children of her own but did raise her niece following the death of Louisa's sister, May, who on her death bed asked Louisa to raise the child. From on-line biography by Deborah Durbin http://xroads.virginia.edu/-hyper/alcott/aboutla.html

Gertrude Bell: Archaeologist, writer, political analyst;
   founder of Baghdad museum
Elizabeth and Emily Blackwell: sisters who were both
   physicians[1]
Nellie Bly: Extraordinary journalist, adventurer
Anne and Emily Bronte: sisters who were both English
   novelists
Mary Cassatt: Artist, Impressionist painter
Emily Dickinson: Poet
Amelia Earhart: Aviator[2]
Elizabeth I: Queen of England
Mary Ann Evans (pen name: George Eliot) English novelist
Lillian Gish: Silent screen actress
Martha Graham: Dancer-choreographer, pioneered modern
   ballet
Alice Hamilton: Pioneer doctor in industrial medicine;
   worked for job safety
Edith Hamilton: Greek scholar, educator, writer
Helen Keller: Blind and deaf author and reformer
Juliette Gordon Low: Founder of the Girl Scouts of America, 1912
Florence Nightingale: Founder of modern nursing
Annie Oakley: Legendary sharpshooter
Adelina Patti: 19th-century opera singer
Anna Pavlova: Famed Russian ballerina
Beatrix Potter: Author of children's books
Jeannette Rankin: First U.S. Congresswoman

---

1 The Blackwell sisters, Elizabeth and Emily, never married or had children. In fact, none of the five Blackwell sisters married; however, they did adopt a few of their servants. They were raised "partly as servants and partly as members of the family." *Blackwell family Papers, 1832-1981: A Finding Aid*, Arthur and Elizabeth Schlesinger Library on the History of Women in America, Radcliffe College, February 1992. http://oasis.lib.harvard.edu/oasis/deliver/-sch00050

2 Amelia Earhart had no children but in 1931 married George Putnam, a divorced man with two sons, born in 1913 and 1921. The older son did pay visits to his father and Amelia in New York, but there is no reason to believe that Amelia ever played 'mom' to his boys, as Putnam's wife, Dorothy, was still living (died 1982). Her reasons for divorce included that she rarely saw her husband and that he failed to provide for their sons. Putnam's career appears to have kept him on the move, and Amelia was quite the globe trotter herself. Amelia disappeared six later (and presumably died). "Amelia Earhart," *Wikipedia* http://en.wikipedia.org/wiki/Amelia_Earhart; and *Amelia and George's Other Marriages and Relationships*, Sheri & Bob Stritof http://marriage.about.com/od/historical/a/ameliaearhart_3.htm

Guilhermina Suggia: Famous woman cellist of the early
   20th century
Ann Sullivan: Helen Keller's teacher and friend
Harriet Tubman: Helped free hundreds of slaves via the
   'Underground Railroad'
Katharine Wright: Aviator, "the Third Wright Brother"
   awarded the French Legion of Honor

Note that this list includes four pairs of sisters, suggesting family backgrounds that were conducive to the development of women's talents. The Bronte sisters were raised by a father who was widowed when his children were very young. His daughters had relatively little experience with the traditional role of women and also were sent away to school.[1]

Maria Gaetana and Maria Teresa d'Agnesi
Elizabeth and Emily Blackwell
Anne and Emily Bronte
Alice and Edith Hamilton

This does not exhaust the list of history's famous women who did not bear children, but is a good sampling. And many of today's successful career women owe a debt of gratitude to these pioneers who opened doors for future generations of women.

Traditionally, men were less restricted than women in the rearing of children, but they too could feel the limitations that biological offspring sometimes placed on their intellectual and creative offspring. Here are just a few of history's famous men who did not sire children:

Alvin Ailey: American choreographer, founded Alvin Ailey
   American Dance Theatre
Francis Bacon: Philosopher
Ludwig van Beethoven: Composer[2]

---

1 *The Bronte sisters on Relationships*, N. Holder, Nov 6, 2011 http://voices.yahoo.com/the-bronte-sisters-relationships-10346871.html
2 Beethoven, upon the death of his brother, helped raised his brother's son. The following is an interesting remark worth noting here: "For nearly two years, Beethoven — then Europe's greatest composer — wrote nothing. Directing his attention toward his nine-year-old nephew simply consumed too much time."

Johannes Brahms: Composer
James Buchanan: President of the United States
Lewis Carroll: Author of *Alice's Adventures in Wonderland*
Frederic Chopin: Composer, pianist[1]
Nicolaus Copernicus: Astronomer, astrologer
Edgar Degas: Artist, French impressionist painter
T.S. Eliot: Poet, editor
George Gershwin: Composer, song writer
Harry Houdini: Magician, escape artist
Langston Hughes: Poet, playwright, novelist
Henry James: Novelist
Immanuel Kant: German philosopher
T.E. Lawrence (Lawrence of Arabia): Adventurer, soldier,
    author, archaeologist
John Stuart Mill: English philosopher
Sir Isaac Newton: Astronomer, physicist, mathematician
Thomas Paine: Author of *The Rights of Man*
Edgar Allan Poe: Short story writer and poet
James K. Polk: President of the United States
Maurice Ravel: Composer, "Bolero"
Gioacchino Rossini: Composer
George Bernard Shaw: Playwright, lecturer
Johann Strauss Jr.: Composer, the "Waltz King"
Henry David Thoreau: Author of *Walden*
Amerigo Vespucci: Explorer and cartographer for whom
    America is named
Leonardo da Vinci: Artist, inventor, scientist
Thornton Wilder: American playwright, Pulitzer Prize
Wilbur and Orville Wright: Aviators
    (See Tables 1 & 2 for hundreds of additional names of
    famous child-free people.)

From *Beethoven and His Nephew*, http://www.awesomestories.com/biographies/beethoven/beethoven-nephew
1 Frederic Chopin never married or had children; however, he did have an affair with the French Novelist Aurore Dudevant, better known as George Sands, who was a divorcée with 2 children. Her children were apparently a factor in the break-up of the Chopin/Sands affair: "However, the tipping point in their relationship involved her daughter Solange. Chopin continued to be cordial to Solange after she and her husband, Auguste Clesinger, had a vicious falling out with Sand over money. Sand took Chopin's support of Solange as outright treachery, and confirmation that Chopin had always "loved" Solange. Sand's son Maurice also disliked Chopin. Maurice wanted to establish himself as the 'man of the estate,' and did not wish to have Chopin as a rival for that role." "George Sands," *Wikipedia*. http://en.wikipedia.org/wiki/George_Sand

---

The addition of a child can place a needless burden on the parents. And this is not to mention the burden procreation places on society as a whole. Past civilizations may not have been as concerned about population growth, deforestation and global warming as those of us living in the 21st century; however, children born in poor health or in poverty have been deemed undesirable by more than one past society. In ancient Greece, when children entered the world as a burden to their parents or to society, the children were left to die or sold into slavery.

In Sparta, "The city-state determined whether babies, both male and female, were strong enough to be Spartan citizens. Infants deemed too weak were abandoned in the countryside to die. Although leaving weak or sickly children to die was common in the Greek world, Sparta made it a part of official government policy."[1]

In Athens, "On occasion, people who owed a lot of money sold themselves or members of their families into slavery to pay off their debts. Sometimes babies were left outside to die if their parents could not take care of them. These infants were often picked up and raised as slaves."[2]

This may seem barbaric, but past generations of Americans sometimes farmed out their children if the cost of raising them was too much of a burden to the family budget. Or parents would abandon their children to orphanages, or even abandon them to the streets. Widowed mothers or fathers would often place their children in orphanages. "By 1910, there were more than 100,000 children in American orphanages."[3]

In the words of Connie DiPasquale, A History of the Orphan Trains, "When the Orphan Train movement began, in the mid-19th century, it was estimated that approximately 30,000 abandoned children were living on the streets of New York."[4] Ms. DiPasquale

---

1 *The Ancient Greeks* by Allison Lassieur, Scholastic Inc. NY 2004, pp.78
2 Ibid., p. 86.
3 *The True History of Orphanages* by F.R. Duplantier, America's Future, 7800 Bonhomme, St. Louis MO 63105 http://www.americasfuture.net/1996/june96/6-16-96b. html
4 *A History of the Orphan Trains* by Connie DiPasquale, *Orphan Trains of Kansas* is contributed by Connie DiPasquale http://www.kancoll.org/articles/orphans/or_hist.htm

cites "massive overpopulation in the New York area due to extensive immigration in the mid 19th century" as one cause of this problem.[1]

She goes on to say that between 150,000 and 200,000 'orphan' children were relocated via the orphan train movement, but that they were not all orphans. "Some children were true orphans, no parents, no other family to look after them, living on the streets, sleeping in doorways, fending for themselves by whatever means necessary. But many of these children had parents. Some were 'half-orphans', one parent had died and the remaining parent could not care for them, so they were placed in an orphanage. Some children still had both parents, but were merely 'turned loose' by the parents because the family had grown too large and they couldn't care for all the children."[2]

Some might argue that this was more barbaric that the Spartan custom of abandoning infants to the countryside to die. The American practice of turning loose their older children often resulted in far more prolonged suffering on the way to death. And those children who did survive knew little or nothing of their heritage, and lived with so much inner turmoil and anger. Their sufferings were multifarious.

There are many brutal reasons for the existence of neglected children on this planet: overpopulation, poverty, death of parents, and war are just a few such reasons. Peer pressure, media pressure and religious pressure all contribute to the problem. Anything that encourages people to have children without giving it a great deal of personal forethought can only aggravate the problem.

One example of this is that old cliché we have all no doubt heard many times in childhood: "When you grow up and get married and have children of your own . . ." This oft' repeated line teaches from an early age that it is a foregone conclusion that all children are expected to procreate as adults. We are brainwashed from childhood into believing that procreation is as unavoidable as taxes and death.

---

1 Ibid.
2 Ibid.

Is it any wonder then that so many children are born from patterns of habit rather than from intelligent introspection?

Society neglects to teach that childbearing is more a responsibility than a right. Unfortunately, far too many people bear children who really are not suited to the occupation of raising children. To argue that everyone should raise children makes as much sense as to argue that everyone should be a doctor, or that everyone should be a secretary, or that everyone should be a concert pianist. Get the picture? People have different talents and different interests. It would be absurd to argue that we should all follow the same line of work. And raising children is work.

Hopefully most people today are enlightened enough to know how important it is to choose a line of work that one likes doing. People are generally best suited for those jobs for which they show an interest. This certainly should apply to raising children. One thing should be obvious: people who see child-rearing as a burden should not so-burden themselves; but the time to think about it is before having children, not after the fact.

CHAPTER 2. DON'T THEY LIKE CHILDREN?

Are child-free people child-haters? Probably no more so than people who have children. Does this sound cynical? It should. But while some child-free adults don't care for the company of children, many child-free people have helped look after nieces, nephews or younger siblings, or have taught school, or otherwise worked with children. They just don't want any of their own for any one of a number of reasons.

On the other hand, many parents don't particularly like children. Indicative of this, many fathers have abandoned their biological offspring; hence, the term: "dead-beat dads." And there have been mothers, too, who have skipped out on their husbands and children when they just couldn't take it anymore. Some parents abuse or neglect their children. And why do parents call their children kids? Isn't this rather demeaning? Parents have the tendency to talk down to their children. Is this a sign of parental dissatisfaction with an irreversible lifestyle choice?

In the mid-seventies there was the disturbing survey carried out by columnist, Ann Landers, which shocked even this experienced advice-giver who thought she'd seen and heard everything. Ms. Landers took an informal survey at the request of one of her readers, and was "flummoxed" to learn that 70% of those who responded regretted having children. There were over 10,000 respondents. She was the first to admit that this survey was not scientific; but it did establish that there are a lot of parents who would not have children if they could do it over again. (The letter and her follow-up interview are discussed in more detail later in this chapter)

When Thales, a pre-Socratic philosopher, was asked why he had no children of his own, he replied "Because I love children."[1] And it may be an anomaly, but it is certainly worth noting here that quite a few authors and illustrators of children's books were child-free, beginning with the late Dr. Seuss, though he became a stepfather when he married his second wife, following the death of his first. But then, he was already in his mid-sixties at the time of his second marriage. Also, among child-free authors are Harriet Potter, creator of Peter Rabbit; and J.M. Barrie, creator of Peter Pan. Hans Christian Anderson was another child-free author of children's stories, as were C.S. Lewis and Lewis Carroll. Louisa May Alcott and Wilson Rawls wrote books for juveniles. Jack Prelutsky has penned books of children's poetry. Maurice Sendak authored and illustrated children's books. So did Crockett Johnson, Emanuele Luzzati and Anne Ophelia Todd Dowden. The British artist, Kate Greenaway, illustrated over 60 children's books and wrote verse for some of these. All of the above were child-free.

Here is a list of some authors of children's books who never had children themselves:

> Louisa May Alcott: *Little Men; Little Women*
> Hans Christian Andersen: *Thumbelina; The Ugly Duckling*
> J.M. Barrie: *Peter Pan*
> Margaret Wise Brown; Authored over a hundred children's
>   books, *Goodnight Moon*
> Lewis Carroll: *Alice's Adventures in Wonderland*

---

1 *Pre-Socratic Philosophy*, by Thomas Knierim, p. 5 "It is said that Thales remained unmarried for all of his life. When his mother pressed him top [sic] marry, he said, 'It is too early', and when he had passed his prime and his mother insisted again, he said, 'It is too late'. When he was asked why he had no children, he would reply, 'Because I love children.'" http://www.thebigview.com/download/greek-philosophy.pdf

C.J. Dennis: Author of children's books of poetry

Kate DiCamillo: *Winn-Dixie*, *The Tiger Rising*

Anne Ophelia Todd Dowden: Botanical artist; authored and illustrated children's books

Gyo Fujikawa: Children's books with multi-racial illustrations before it was politically correct

Theodor Seuss Geisel a.k.a. "Dr Seuss": *The Cat in the Hat*

Kate Greenaway: British artist, illustrated over 60 children's books

Crockett Johnson: Illustrator of children's books; Cartoonist, "Barnaby"

Ruth Krauss: *The Carrot Seed*

C.S. Lewis: *The Lion, the Witch and the Wardrobe*

Emanuele Luzzati: Artist, illustrator of children's books

Rose O'Neill: Artist, illustrator, wrote children's books, invented the Kewpie Doll

Michelle Paver: *Wolf Brother, Spirit Walker*

Beatrix Potter: *Peter Rabbit*

Jack Prelutsky: Author of children's poems, "children's poet laureate"

Wilson Rawls: *Where the Red Fern Grows*

Maurice Sendak: Author and illustrator of children's books. *Where the Wild Things Are*

Kay Thompson: Author of children's books, *Eloise*

Elizabeth Janet Gray Vining: *Meggy MacIntosh*; *Adam of the Road*

This list should give one something to ponder. These authors expressed themselves through creation rather than procreation. An author's book is often referred to as his "brainchild." Creative people have that 'inner child' that often replaces any desire for a biological child. Is it possible then that a biological child is often a substitute for creative self-expression? Is this why so many parents try to relive their lives through their own children?

And while on the subject of children's books, it's worth noting how many fairy tales end with the prince and princess finding one another and living happily ever after, but without mention of their having children: e.g., Cinderella, Snow White, Sleeping Beauty. Fairy tales stop short of the prince and princess procreating. Then on the other hand, there is the nursery rhyme about the old woman who lived in a shoe, who had so many children she didn't know what to do. This rhyme certainly does not conjure up the romantic imagery of the above-mentioned fairy tales. Were these early fairy tales and rhymes a secret longing for a child-free life in a time pre-dating modern birth control?

So there are child-free folks who like children, and parents who don't. But in all probability, most regretful parents don't hate their children—they simply regret that they made this their lifestyle choice.

Also, there are still many people alive today who have painful memories of shotgun weddings, illegitimate births, homes for un-wed mothers, and orphanages full of unadopted children. These were some of the sad signs of children whose biological parents would rather not have brought them into the world. The 1960s ushered in the sexual revolution via the introduction of "the pill," followed by legalized abortion in the 1970s. And today, one seldom hears anymore of shotgun weddings. Yet even with today's birth control options, there are many parents who envy their child-free friends.

While today's children are less likely to be accidents of birth, there are parents who regret their decision to have children. Society simply did not prepare them for this choice. The media would still have you believe that children are a bundle of joy, but fail to make clear the responsibilities and sacrifices involved in parenting.

Post-impressionist artist Paul Gauguin (1848–1903) is an exam-ple of a man who was not prepared for the responsibilities of family life and so sacrificed his family for his art. "By 1884 Gauguin had moved with his family to Copenhagen, where he pursued a busi-ness career as a stockbroker. Driven to paint full-time, he returned to Paris in 1885, leaving his family in Denmark. Without adequate subsistence, his wife (Mette Sophie Gadd) and their five children returned to her family. Gauguin outlived two of his children.[1]

Did he have a moral right to abandon his family? Probably not. But had he not chosen his art over his family, then the world would

---

1 Paul Gauguin Biography. This website is licensed under a Creative Commons License Copyright © 2002-2014 http://www.paul-gauguin.net/biography.html

have been deprived of his work. Gauguin also fathered several children by mistresses. He certainly did not qualify for any father-of-the-year awards and serves to illustrate why it is best for people to find themselves first, before starting a family, or they may "find themselves" when it is too late. One's true calling in life may not be compatible with rearing a family.

In returning to the subject matter of this chapter, the question of whether child-free people don't like children: one common complaint of the child-free is that too many parents don't teach their children manners, and allow their children to be noisy and disorderly in public places such as restaurants, stores and theaters. But isn't it the parents, not the children, who should be the objects of scorn when they fail to teach and discipline their children? There are situations in which parents need to be reminded of these old words of wisdom:

"Children should be seen but not heard."

And it's certainly understandable that child-free folks resent having to put up with crying babies in adjacent apartments. Tenants are required to sign rental agreements that they will keep their noise confined to within their own walls; but how do you make a crying baby understand this? If parents believe in letting their babies cry themselves to sleep, what about the neighbors who need their sleep? And then there are noisy teenagers with their boom boxes and loud car radios. It is no wonder if child-free people resent children; but this anger should be redirected at the parents instead.

Past generations of child-free people suffered, generally in silence, the discrimination against them; but today's child-free couples and individuals are fighting back. Today, there is a fair amount of friction between people with children and people without, judging from all the child-free web sites and from the web sites defending parenthood. For instance, parents often argue that child-free people are selfish; but one can certainly argue the selfishness of having children. Child-free web sites refer to parents as 'breeders' or worse. The other side posts hostile comments about child-free folks. And child-free couples with pets have often been accused of substituting pets for children; but have you ever witnessed parents walking their small children on a leash? What might one say about this? Touché!

Parents who regret having children differ from child-free folks in one crucially important way: child-free people know that they don't wish to have children; whereas regretful parents learn only after the fact that they don't want children. This is one lesson you don't want to learn the hard way.

The Ann Landers Survey

Now let's look at that legendary letter that appeared in Ms. Lander's column[1] and her follow-up interview in *Good Housekeeping Magazine*:

If You Had It To Do Over Again— Would You Have Children?

Ms. Landers explains that she received a letter from a young woman about to be married. She and her fiancé were trying to decide if they wanted to have children. Here is the letter that started it all:

> "So many of our friends," the letter said, "seem to resent their children. They envy us our freedom to go and come as we please. Then there's the matter of money. They say their kids keep them broke. One couple we know had their second child in January. Last week, she had her tubes tied and he had a vasectomy—just to make sure. All this makes me wonder, Ann Landers. Is parenthood worth the trouble? Jim and I are very much in love. Our relationship is beautiful. We don't want anything to spoil it. All around us we see couples who were so much happier before they were tied down with a family. Will you please ask your readers the question: If you had it to do over again, would you have children?"[2]

---

1 Ann Landers is Copyright Creators Syndicate, Inc.

2 More than one web site erroneously states that the Ann Landers column, "If You Had It To Do Over Again—Would You Have Children?" appeared on November 3, 1975. Searching a number of major city newspapers, we see the *Seattle Post Intelligencer* of that date (p.B2) posts a letter entitled, "Can Kids Ruin Happy Old Age?" But this letter begins, "My husband and I have been married for a year and are undecided as to whether or not we should have children." It is not the letter quoted by Ms. Landers in the June 1976 *Good Housekeeping* and in the PDF (http://www.stats.uwo.ca/faculty/bellhouse/stat353annlanders.pdf) a project

In a follow-up interview that appeared in Good Housekeeping (June 1976), Miss Landers states that she printed the letter and was overwhelmed by both the number of replies and the number of parents who replied "No."[1] "After five days of reading, counting, and sorting mail, a bleary-eyed staff of eight secretaries announced we had received over 10,000 responses, and—are you ready for this?—70 percent of those who wrote said, 'No. If I had it to do over again, I would not have children.'"

She heard from parents, young and old, cutting across social classes. The letters poured in from such diverse locations as Anchorage, San Antonio, Boston and Kentucky. This letter had struck "an unprecedented number of raw nerves. The question unleashed an incredible torrent of confessions—'things I could never tell anyone else...'" She heard from welfare moms and from the well-to-do.

Of the more than 10,000 responses, Ms. Landers states that about 40% of the parents who said that they would not have children if they could do it over again did not sign their names, but nearly all of those who said that they would still have children did sign their names, and many of the latter gave Ms. Landers permission to use their names. It is understandable that the "no" voters were reluctant to disclose their names. It is not easy for regretful parents to admit even to themselves, let alone openly, that parenting was a mistake.

Ms. Landers goes on to say:

> Approximately 80 percent of the total response came from women. The average letter ran almost a page longer than the usual Landers letter. I was particularly moved by the intensity of feeling.

> Dozens who wrote said, "I am weeping as I write this. It's the first time I have ever put such thoughts about my children down on paper. It's painful."

Many of the "no" voters did sign their names but asked Ms. Landers not to respond, apparently from fear or embarrassment of having their letters discovered by family members. Wrote one

---

of the University of Western Ontario which helps to explain the confusion. The popular letter widely circulated online was submitted to Ms. Landers some couple months later.

1 *Good Housekeeping*, June 1976, pp.100, 101, 215, 216, 223, 224.

respondent: "Please don't answer in any way, shape or form." Ms. Landers found that the "no" votes could be divided mainly into four categories. Let's examine these.

Category One: Her first category included people concerned about world problems such as overpopulation, world hunger and nuclear weapons. One letter came from a man who wrote, "The world is in lousy shape. We would feel guilty if we brought a child into this mess."

How many parents debated their procreative urge versus world problems before having children? Is this why some child-free couples have abstained from procreating: Universal considerations took precedence over personal interests?

Category Two: This included parents who stated that children ruined their marriage. "'Our happiest years were the ones before the babies came,' wrote an Atlanta woman. 'In those days, we had time for the theater, parties, rides in the country, weekend trips and best of all—each other.' A wife who had signed her letter 'Too Late For Tears in Tampa' wrote, 'I was a successful, attractive, career woman before I had these kids. Now I'm an exhausted, shrieking, nervous wreck—too tired for sex, conversation or anything else.'" And from a Chicago mom: "The price of food is out of sight. My husband was laid off for six weeks last winter and we had to accept help from my folks. It was humiliating. We love our kids but they are so damned expensive. Actually they haven't given us that much pleasure. We'd have to vote 'no.'"

Let's update Category Two with a few online comments from a blog by Carolyn Robertson, Has motherhood hurt your marriage? "A recent study in the *Journal of Marriage and Family* looks into why so many women—40%, they say—report a decline in marital happiness after they become mothers. A lot of it comes down to time: Couples with kids spend 2 hours less a day together than those without them."[1]

---

1 "Has motherhood hurt your marriage?" By Carolyn Robertson (babycenter blog) http://blogs.babycenter.com/mom_stories/has-motherhood-hurt-your-marriage/

The Website of Dr. Mark Goulston states that, "Children DO cause divorce." "When I've asked couples I have seen in marital therapy (realize they are seeing me because they have problems) how their relationship was before they had children, most will say that it was happier."[1]

And from the blog "Hollywood Life" by Bonnie Fuller, *Crying Babies In The Middle Of The Night End One In Three Marriages*: "According to a new study, one-third of married couples with children will split due to sleepless nights — because their screaming babies keep them up! . . . There are many reasons why marriages end, but a new study claims crying babies are a major cause for parents splitting up! The study, conducted by the show Bedtime Live on British TV station Channel 4, polled 2,000 parents about how much sleep they get each night, and the reason for their lack of sleep."[2]

Returning to the Ann Landers article:

Category Three: Ms. Landers stated that these "contained the most pathetic letters of all. They came from older parents whose children had grown up and left home. 'Manhattan Mom' wrote with more rancor than self-pity. 'I get a postcard from the Bahamas at Christmastime. On Mother's Day, I get an azalea plant. In between, maybe two phone calls. I raised that boy alone. His father died of cancer when he was three. Some thanks I get.'"

This last letter illustrates the attitude of many parents that their children owe them something for having been brought into this world. Compare this comment with the earlier one from the man in Category One who wrote that he would feel guilty "if we brought a child into this mess." Just what do children owe their parents? What do parents owe their children? Did the parents choose to have children? Did the children choose to be born? See Chapter Eight, A Right Not to Be Born, for further discussion of this.

Category Four: This included letters from parents whose children were in trouble with the law. "'Where are the joys of parenthood?' asked a Washington, D.C., mother. 'We haven't seen them.

---

1 The website of Dr. Mark Goulston: http://markgoulston.com/ usable-insight-children-do-cause-divorce/

2 "Hollywood Life" by Bonnie Fuller, March 18, 2013. http://hollywoodlife. com/2013/03/18/screaming-kids-divorce-reason-study/#

But we've seen a good deal of security guards who've caught our daughter shoplifting. We have also seen policemen who picked up our youngest son for selling drugs on the school grounds. We've seen some very depressing emergency rooms where the older boys were taken by an ambulance after totaling two cars and one motorcycle.'"

Can Category Four problems be blamed on single moms? According to Jason DeParle and Sabrina Tavernise in *The New York Times*, "For Women Under 30, Most Births Occur Outside Marriage." The article goes on to say, "The shift is affecting children's lives. Researchers have consistently found that children born outside marriage face elevated risks of falling into poverty, failing in school or suffering emotional and behavioral problems."[1]

And from Rainbows, an international non-profit organization for helping children, "Gang recruitment is a powerful lure for the products of broken homes and single-parent households."[2]

Some juvenile delinquents come from "good family backgrounds" but the odds of juvenile crime increase when children are raised in single parent households. The National Criminal Justice Reference Service (NCJRS) cites The Journal of Research in Crime and Delinquency as saying, "the most reliable indicator of violent crime in a community is the proportion of fatherless families. Fathers typically offer economic stability, a role model for boys, greater household security, and reduced stress for mothers. This is especially true for families with adolescent boys, the most crime-prone cohort. Children from single-parent families are more prone than children from two-parent families to use drugs, be gang members, be expelled from school, be committed to reform institutions, and become juvenile murderers. Single parenthood inevitably reduces the amount of time a child has in interaction with someone who is

---

1 *The New York Times*, "For Women Under 30, Most Births Occur Outside Marriage" by Jason DeParle and Sabrina Tavernise, Feb 17, 2012. http://www.nytimes.com/2012/02/18/us/for-women-under-30-most-births-occur-outside-marriage.html?pagewanted=all

2 *Rainbows* http://www.rainbows.org/statistics.html. (Rainbows cites the 1995 Chicago Crime Commission Report as its source.)

attentive to the child's needs, including the provision of moral guidance and discipline."[1]

So children raised by divorced or unwed mothers are more likely to get into trouble with the law, but ironically it is the children who are sometimes the cause of divorce. And if unwed moms think they don't have to worry about divorce, their children could still be the cause of a failed relationship, especially if the man in that relationship is not the biological father. But why this trend of unwed mothers? We will revisit this question in Chapter Nine, World Karma.

In returning to Ms. Landers: she goes on to say that she believes many parents are disappointed because their children failed to live up to the parents' expectations and because, "Too many parents have a grossly unrealistic approach to parenthood." Ms. Landers, herself a mother, asks, "Are there some invisible components to help explain that staggering 70-percent negative response? Some missing pieces to the puzzle? I see one, for sure. The person who is against something rather than for it is much more readily inclined to take pen in hand and express his anxiety, rage, or disappointment. People who are contented are rarely motivated to write and tell me how happy they are. Anger, hostility and resentment are often the fuel that moves people to action."

Parents may be disappointed in their children; nevertheless, parental discontent with one's progeny is not an acceptable excuse for divorce. If two people want out of a relationship, the time to do so is before having children. When people choose to procreate, they have responsibility to their children and to society and must put aside some of their own personal interests. People who are not prepared to do so are not prepared to be good parents. Society makes it too easy for parents to divorce, and many parents never marry in the first place. For unwed couples, perhaps the birth of a child should count as wedding vows in the eyes of the law.

A marriage is between two people—until those two people become three or more. Children are not property, and parents should not get away with putting their own interests ahead of the interests

---

1 NCJRS, National Criminal Justice Reference Service https://www.ncjrs.gov/App/Publications/abstract.aspx?ID=167327

of their children. Ironically, today when people have the freedom to be child-free, many people still have children and live to regret it.

One litmus test to be put to potential parents is how they have cared for their pets. People who have abandoned their animals or given them away or taken them to the pound have demonstrated that they are not mature enough for parenting. Cats and dogs have feelings as sensitive as a human and they need to be adopted by individuals mature enough to commit to caring for them for the lifetime of the animal.

If you get rid of your pet when it is no longer convenient to keep it, then, chances are, you will tire of your children when you find them to be an inconvenience. You may well join those 70% who would not have children if they could do it over again.

We have Ms. Landers to thank for opening the door to a subject that was previously taboo. No subject so important as whether to have children should remain behind locked doors.

CHAPTER 3. QUESTIONS AND ANSWERS

Child-free individuals and couples are frequently asked the same repetitious questions, and hear the same trite arguments. While some people ask these questions sincerely, without intended rudeness, other folks have every intention of being rude; and it's not always that easy to differentiate between the former and the latter. For the edification of the former, these questions are worth answering. As for the latter, no answers will satisfy these people since they often are asking from a position of envy and regret.

Questions:
> Don't you like children?
> What if your parents had never had children?
> Don't you care about your family name?
> Don't you want genetic immortality?
> Who will take care of you when you are old?

First question: "Don't you like children?"
Answer: See previous chapter.

Second question: "What if your parents had never had children?"

Answer: This question is truly a no-brainer, and one that is difficult to answer with a straight face. Obviously, if your parents had never had children, they would not be parents and you would not be here to answer such a dumb question. If you never existed, then you obviously would not have the consciousness to care whether you existed. This is Descarte's axiom in reverse. "I think; therefore I am" becomes "If I am not, then I don't think."

Third question: "What about your family name?"

Answer: If you're a woman, with or without children, you aren't likely to carry the family name forward. So this is a sexist question. If you're a man, you may have brothers who'll carry the name forward, and if not brothers, perhaps cousins. Most names are not that rare and will survive with or without your help.

Fourth question: "Don't you want genetic immortality?"

Answer: This is indirectly what the previous question is really asking. In Greek mythology, when Medea killed her own children, she was trying to destroy her husband's immortality. Some ancient civilizations believed that you are immortal through your children and their descendants. Let's examine this argument. First, if your immortality requires an unbroken line of descendants, then having children does not assure immortality. Your children may not carry the genetic code forward. If you have enough children, then you'll likely have grandchildren; however, if everyone subscribes to that philosophy, then we get overpopulation: the problem we face now. And overpopulation threatens the very existence of our species — and thus ends the unbroken line of descendants.

And there is another way of achieving immortality: through great accomplishments. Mozart had children; Beethoven had none. Do you know the names of Mozart's children? Probably not; but you know the name, Mozart. And chances are, you've heard his immortal music. Now ask yourself this: Is Beethoven any less immortal than Mozart?

Fifth question: "Who will take care of you when you are old?"

Answer: Hopefully, you will be able to take care of yourself; however, the reality is that many folks are not able to do so, and they end up in nursing homes or assisted living arrangements or some other type of institution. This is truly an American tragedy, as our nation is bulging with nursing homes full of discarded old folks. And many of these forgotten old folks have children who are not around, or who come to visit their parents only when they can fit it into their schedules. Modern society is highly mobile, with people frequently re-locating. Big business is a culprit here, as big business often relocates employees. This was far less a problem when people worked for small companies and were more likely to stay put.

All these neglected elderly folks constitute such a sad state of affairs that it's indecent to even joke about it. It is shameful to see how our society discards its elders in their so-called golden years. But the point here is that having children is no guarantee that this won't happen to you.

Now let's examine some of the arguments which child-free folks hear.

If no one had children the human race would die out.

Children are our future.

There aren't enough white babies being born.

Your child might accomplish something really important.

Childbearing is a woman's greatest achievement.

Your parents want grandchildren.

You were a baby once.

The only reason for getting married is to have children.

Your biological clock is ticking.

You'll change your mind.

It's selfish not to have children.

First argument: "If no one had children the human race would die out."

Rebuttal: This is true, of course; but if too many people have children the human race may die out. Right now, overpopulation, not underpopulation, is a far greater threat to human existence and to other life on this planet as well.

Second argument: "Children are our future."
Rebuttal: If there are too many of them, the human race may not have a future. Also, how often have we heard that "children are our future" as if future generations should solve the problems that the present population has created? Isn't it time we solve our own problems instead of leaving that to future generations?

Third argument: "There aren't enough white babies being born."
Rebuttal: This sure sounds racist. Perhaps some white folks are afraid to find out what it's like when the shoe is on the other foot. According to Pew Research Social and Demographic Trends (May 17, 2012): "Among Hispanics, the total fertility rate is 2.4. For non-Hispanic whites and for non-Hispanic Asians, it is 1.8. Non-Hispanic blacks (2.1) have higher fertility than whites but lower fertility than Hispanics."[1] This having been said, white babies born in the U.S. have a longer life expectancy than black or Hispanic babies born in the U.S.[2, 3] This may be owing to the white population's smaller family size. Children raised in financially deprived households average a shorter life expectancy than those from more affluent backgrounds. And it stands to reason that families with large numbers of children are more likely to suffer financial hardships: the cost of raising a child today is prohibitive. So couples who are having large numbers of children are more likely to have short-lived children.

Fourth argument: "Your child might accomplish something really important."

1 Pew Research Social and Demographic Trends (May 17, 2012): Explaining Why Minority Births Now Outnumber White Births by Jeffrey S. Passel, Gretchen Livingston and D'Vera Cohn http://www.pewsocialtrends.org/2012/05/17/explaining-why-minority-births-now-outnumber-white-births/
2 National Center for Health Statistics [U.S.]. http://www.cdc.gov/nchs/fastats/lifexpec.htm
3 Daily News Central, *Health News*, Sept 12, 2006. "Race, Income, Geography Influence U.S. Life Expectancy" by Tom Harrison. http://health.dailynewscentral.com/content/view/0002418/42/. According to a Harvard study, and based upon factors such as race, geography and income, Asian Americans have the longest life expectancy (84.9), followed by white Americans (75–79 based on income and geography), and then black Americans (71.1–72.9 based on income and geography).

Rebuttal: Statistically, don't bet on it. You could also have a child who turns out to be a criminal. Most people, however, are neither geniuses nor criminals, though there seems to be more of the latter than the former. Also, we might all be living in a much better world if people would work on fulfilling their own aspirations instead of placing that burden on their children.

And as a matter of statistics, according to Wikipedia, the online encyclopedia, "The United States has the highest documented incarceration rate, and total documented prison population in the world. As of year-end 2007, a record 7.2 million people were behind bars, on probation or on parole. Of the total, 2.3 million were incarcerated. More than 1 in 100 American adults were incarcerated at the start of 2008."[1]

"More than 1 in 100 American adults" does not even address the issue of juvenile offenders. Nor do the above-cited statistics include ex-cons who have served their time and are no longer on probation. These statistics also fail to include the criminal element of society which has managed to evade the law and prosecution. With so many crimes going unsolved, that number is no doubt large.

Think about that the next time you try to argue, "Your child might accomplish something really important." Then, too, there are all those parents who are just plain disappointed that their children did not turn out to be the spitting image of themselves.

Fifth argument: "Childbearing is a woman's greatest achievement."

Rebuttal: Tell that to Florence Nightingale, Susan B. Anthony, Helen Keller, or any of the other remarkable women whose names appear in this work. To say that childbearing is a woman's greatest achievement is an extraordinarily sexist remark. How many people would say that Mozart's greatest achievement was siring children?

---

1 *Wikipedia* Incarceration in the United States (Redirected from Prisons in the United States) http://en.wikipedia.org/wiki/Prisons_in_the_United_States *International Journal of Epidemiology*, May 9, 2006. "Widening socioeconomic inequalities in US life expectancy, 1980–2000." Also, "Those in less-deprived groups experienced a longer life expectancy at each age than their counterparts in more-deprived groups." http://ije.oxfordjournals.org/cgi/content/full/35/4/969.

Sixth argument: "Your parents want grandchildren."

Rebuttal: It's not your responsibility to bring people into this world to please someone else. The fact that your parents had you does not require that you give them grandchildren. Your parents made their own life-choices, and you have the right to make yours.

Seventh argument: "You were a baby once."

Rebuttal: Weren't we all! So what's your point? To the best of our knowledge, we don't ask to be born. Your parents, not you, are responsible for your entry into this world. If you have children, then you are responsible for their entry into this world.

Eighth argument: "The only reason for getting married is to have children."

Rebuttal: No, it's not! People have married for various reasons, though not all admirable: love, money, citizenship, fame, to name a few. But on the other hand, one might put forth some valid arguments for why people should marry if they plan on having children.

Ninth argument: "Your biological clock is ticking."

Rebuttal: Do you think having children will make it stop ticking? Seriously, what this argument means is that if you delay having children, it may be too late when you get around to it. This is a possibility; however; there's a difference between delaying and not wanting. If a couple hope to have children someday but are not prepared to do so at the present moment, they may find out, when they are ready for children, that indeed time has run out for them; but childfree couples don't want children now or later.

And here's an interesting comment about biological clocks and children by astrophysicist Martin Rees: "In a sense because I've never been athletic and because I've never had children that probably means I'm less oriented age-wise than some people. I'm 60 but I don't really feel any different from when I was 30."[1]

Tenth argument: "You'll change your mind."

---

1 http://www.guardian.co.uk/life/interview/story/0,12982,941906,00.html

Rebuttal: It's possible; but people with children may change their minds too, and there's not a darn thing they can do about it. Childfree people are generally satisfied with their decision; but many parents have lived to regret their choice.

Eleventh argument: "It's selfish not to have children."

Rebuttal: What could be more selfish than to create a life to please one's self? Since to the best of our knowledge we are born without our consent, it is truly an act of selfishness to bring people into this world to satisfy one's own objectives. And just what are these objectives? Is this a hidden wish to control another person, to make property of another person? How close is a child to being property? When parents engage in custody battles, is this really a battle over property rights — my genes vs. your genes? If the battling parents could withdraw their respective genes from the child would the battle be the same? Is procreation the drive for genetic immortality? And how many parents can honestly say that they have not tried to determine the lifestyle, religion, politics, or relationships of their children? Do people who desire children ever bring them into this world without having some selfish motive? If you have no selfish motives for procreating, then you don't want children.

What's wrong with wanting personal freedom? We're taught in this society that we should be willing to die for freedom (the argument often used for going to war). And in the mid-20th century, the catch phrase was "better dead than red." If freedom is this important then why on earth would one want to undermine one's own freedom through procreation? Parents may desire to control the lives of their children, but it is the children who control the lives of their parents.

CHAPTER 4. THE PROCREATION – I.Q. CONNECTION

Is it smart to have children? Or to paraphrase, do smart people have children? Certainly you can find examples of smart people who have children; but on a per capita basis, are smart people less likely to have children? Smart people tend to have fewer children.[1] And studies have also shown that people with fewer children tend to have smarter children.[2]

One argument is that with fewer children each child gets more parental attention. But to play devil's advocate: in today's busy society, often both parents work and so children receive less parental attention than when mothers stayed home. So even with today's smaller family size, children may be receiving less parental attention per child than what was customary in earlier generations with larger families. Also to be considered is quality vs. quantity. Are a few well-spent hours of parental guidance more valuable than a larger number of inferior guidance-hours?

---

1 Lynn, Richard: Eugenics/dysgenics: *Dysgenics: Genetic Deterioration in Modern Populations*; Praeger, 1996. "Professor Lynn surveys studies from all over the world, and everywhere finds the least intelligent people having the most children."http://www.eugenics.net/papers/lynnrev.html

2 Greenberg, Joel: "Family size tied to SAT, IQ scores"; *Science News* June 1, 1985. http://www.articlearchives.com/education-training/academic-standards-testing/250144-1.html

And doesn't it stand to reason that if smart people have fewer children, and if having fewer children means smarter children, that this is because they are the progeny of smarter parents: hence, smarter children? In other words, is it the case that the children are smarter not necessarily because they have fewer siblings, but because they have smarter parents. And because they have smarter parents they also have fewer siblings?

Where A = smarter parents; and B = fewer children; and C = smarter children, it's not necessarily the case that A causes B and B causes C. But isn't it also possible that A does cause both B and C?

And aren't there other factors to consider? Why the tendency to seek one common denominator to answer complex questions? Often there are multiple factors that reinforce or off-set one another. For instance, with fewer children, a family's finances may be in better shape, providing a better home environment for the children, including better nutrition. But this too is debatable since lack of money is not the only reason for poor diet in our society. Too many Americans, who can afford to eat better, fill their diets with junk food and food on-the-go. The middle class often suffers malnutrition for lack of time rather than lack of money.

What about playmates? What influence do they have on a child's learning ability? And teachers? There is quite a range in quality of schools. And parents with fewer children may be better equipped to finance a higher quality education for their children than if they had opted for a larger family. But here, too, is room for argument, as education is not just limited to the academic realm and comes in many forms. So does intelligence for that matter. And some geniuses did not attend college, nor have much public schooling. So authorities may be too narrow in their measurements of intelligence, trying to standardize such measurements based on the homogenization of society; but this homogenization can destroy the individuality from which genius so often derives.

And to turn the whole matter on its head: genius sometimes springs from humble beginnings, whereas too much comfort can lead to complacency and mediocrity. 'Spoiled brats' may develop better financial skills and earning capacity than children raised lower down on the economic scale, but this does not mean that the former have better minds or morals.

Thus far, the discussion here has focused on how parental intelligence and family size influence the intelligence of the children; but what about the influence children have on the intelligence of their parents? Parents may learn from helping their children with homework; but, overall, do children's needs limit the time that parents have for developing their own talents and fulfilling their own creative needs? Do children stunt the intellectual or creative growth of their parents?

The answer here appears to be yes, as many parents seem to have little to talk about other than their children. And how many parents have used their children as an excuse for not being more engaged in civic responsibilities — for not having the time? How many parents do you know who were more interesting conversationalists, and more gung ho to solve world problems, before babies entered the picture, shifting their perspective? Often, parents' views of the world tend to be seen through their children's needs rather than through global issues.

With or without children, we all get twenty-four hours to a day. It's not easy juggling family, career, and social consciousness within that time-frame; and social consciousness is, itself, an important form of education. Intelligent people tend to have a global consciousness; however, overpopulation is one global issue that many parents prefer to avoid discussing if they themselves have contributed to the problem. Or if they do engage in a discussion of the matter, they tend to be in denial; but in today's world, overpopulation leaves no room for intelligent denial of the problem.

Coming at it from a somewhat different angle, eugenics, the study of improving human traits through selective breeding: this is a science with frightening possibilities. While there may be general agreement about wanting to improve the quality of humankind, this also conjures up visions of the horrors of Hitler's idea of the perfect race, and the experiments of Josef Mengele, who tortured and murdered thousands of Jews and others in trying to create that 'perfect' race. So selective breeding should certainly be cause for great concern. And who's to decide what these higher qualities should be anyway?

Nonetheless, there is legitimate concern that if people of lesser intelligence have larger families than people of higher intelligence, then the human race has a dismal future. Even in the 1930s, this concern was being expressed here in the United States:

"WYNNE SEES PERIL IN BIRTH CONTROL" reads the title of a 1936 article in the *New York Times*, with the following subtitle: "Fears Lowered Intelligence Because the Wrong People Have Large Families." This article goes on to say, "Continuance of birth control by the healthy and intelligent, and with population increases coming from the mentally and physically unfit, will soon lower the average intelligence of the United States to less than 10 years of age, Dr. Shirley W. Wynne, former Commissioner of Health of New York City, warned yesterday."[1]

Granted, many of today's young adults do behave like ten-year-olds, with their addiction to cellphones and other gadgetry; however, this dumbing down of America seems more the result of material excess and negligent parenting than the result of birth control. Americans of more mature age grew up with far less materialism, but far better upbringing and behavior. So it would appear that parents with more money to lavish on their children are doing an inferior job of raising their progeny. Two-income families might produce better-behaved offspring if the parents would decide which one will stay home and raise the children. If neither parent wants this responsibility, then why on earth are they having children?

If people of low intelligence are having more children than people of higher intelligence this could be a problem; however, our society has some rethinking to do about what constitutes intelligence. Perhaps there's too much tendency to measure intelligence based on income when we should be measuring intelligence on qualities such as honesty, integrity and concern for the environment. There is certainly nothing intelligent about the way in which American excess is harming the planet. So is income being misused as a measure of intelligence?

---

1 *The New York Times*, Sunday April 19, 1936, section 1, p.25.

Chapter 5. Child-free and the Professions

Geniuses are often child-free, and sometimes they seem to exist in a different realm from the general population because true genius is driven almost by possession, which should not be confused with the common desire for fame and fortune. For example, if you fancy yourself a writer, do you find yourself at a loss for something to write about, or do you have ideas that are just bursting to get out of your head and an overwhelming urge to capture these on paper? A writer does not say to himself, "I want to be a writer." A writer is a writer.

Likewise, the artist is driven to express himself through his chosen field of music, dance or painting. (Though it may be that the field chose him. Or, of course, her.) Many people are drawn to the so-called glamour professions, and simply want to see their name up in lights; but the true artist, the creative genius, has a much higher calling than mere fame. To be born with the soul of an artist and fail is to self-destruct. The same is likely true of great geniuses in most any field: e.g., architecture or science.

The standard Homo sapiens blueprint is birth, maturity, procreation and death — the cycle we share with other animal species. But for the genius, genetic reproduction is not always that important, as the true genius is here to bring forth something other than just more people into this world.

Quite a few of the world's great composers were child-free (and, no, they were not all gay); and of those composers who did sire children, they were not always the best fathers. And their progeny were the consequence of the father's libido rather than the father's genius. It is fair to say that some geniuses who had children may not have done so if today's birth control options had been available to them.

By profession, here are some artists, scientists, writers, social reformers and others who did not procreate, listed under Actors/Actresses; Adventurers (explorers, daring risk takers); Architects; Artists; Cartoonists; Champion Athletes; Comedians; Dancers/Choreographers; Fashion Designers; Film makers/directors; Food-related personalities; Founders; Historians; Inventors; Journalists, news reporters, editors; Judges; Lyricists; Mathematicians; Music: Classical Musicians; Music: Composers; Music: Conductors; Music: Opera singers; Music: Popular singers/musicians; Nobel Prize winners; Notable educators; Philanthropists; Philosophers; Pioneer physicians; Political and world leaders; Scientists; Social reformers; Talk show hosts; Writers; Miscellaneous categories of notable people; and Centenarians:

Actors/Actresses:

Tallulah Bankhead: Movie actress
Theda Bara: Silent screen actress, honored on US postage stamp
Kathy Bates: Oscar winning actress
Jacqueline Bisset: Movie actress
Ray Bolger: Actor, entertainer, Scarecrow in *Wizard of Oz*
Louise Brooks: Actress in silent movies
Betty Buckley: Movies, TV, Broadway: *Cats*
Stockard Channing: Stage and screen
George Clooney: Hollywood Movies
Dolores Del Rio: Mexican-American film actress
Dame Edith Evans: British stage actress

Lynn Fontanne: Actress of American theatre over 40
years
Greta Garbo: Movies
Ava Gardner: Movies
Lillian Gish: Silent screen actress
George "Gabby" Hayes: Vaudeville, Hollywood westerns
Katherine Hepburn: Movies
Souad Hosni: Egyptian movie actress
Ben Johnson: Hollywood movies
DeForest Kelley: Popular TV series, *Star Trek*
Myrna Loy: Movies
Helen Mirren: Academy Award winning actress
Paul Muni: Hollywood and Broadway
Barry Nelson: First actor to play James Bond
Guy Pearce: Australian actor
Claude Piéplu: French actor; activist for nuclear
disarmament
Suzanne Pleshette: Movies and TV
Anne Revere: Broadway (Tony winner); Hollywood (3 Os-
car nominations)
Holland Taylor: Theatre, TV, films
Christopher Walken: movies
Mae West: Movies

Adventurers (explorers, daring risk takers) who did not sire/bear children:

Robert Abram Bartlett: Arctic explorer; first to sail north of
88 degrees north latitude
Olav Olavson Bjaaland: Polar explorer with first group to
reach South Pole, and champion skier
Nellie Bly (a.k.a. Elizabeth Cochrane): Extraordinary jour-
nalist, adventurer
Kalpana Chawla: Astronaut
Amelia Earhart: Aviator
Mary Jayne Gold: Rescued Jewish and anti-Nazi artists
from occupied France
Sven Hedin: Explorer, geographer, who mapped central
Asia; found remains of lost cities
Harry Houdini: Escape artist
T.E. Lawrence (Lawrence of Arabia): Adventurer, soldier,
author, archaeologist

Meriwether Lewis: Explorer, "Lewis and Clark"
Harriet Quimby: Pioneer aviator, first American woman to
earn a pilot's license and pilot the English Channel.
Sally Ride: Astronaut
Harriet Tubman: Escaped slave who helped free others
Amerigo Vespucci: Explorer and cartographer for whom
America is named
Nancy Wake: WWII Decorated spy for the Allies

Architects who did not sire/bear children:

Marion Lucy Mahony Griffin: Artist, architect; worked for
Frank Lloyd Wright
Walter Burley Griffin: International architect; designed
Canberra (Capitol of Australia)
Thomas Hastings: Architect: "Carrère and Hastings" (built
NY library)
Ralph Knott: Architect who built the Edwardian Baroque
style County Hall, London
Charles Rennie Mackintosh: Architect and painter Scotland
England
Edgar A. Tafel: Award winning architect, designed church-
es, college campuses
George Wightwick: Prominent English architect and archi-
tectural journalist

Artists who did not sire/bear children:

Jean Béraud: French Impressionist painter
William Blake: English artist, engraver, poet
Rosa Bonheur: French painter of animals
Michelangelo Buonarroti: Italian Renaissance artist; paint-
ed ceiling of Sistine Chapel
Reuben Bussey: English artist, oils, watercolors, sketches,
portraits and landscapes
Mary Cassatt: American impressionist painter
Nicholas Chevalier: Russian born painter, lithographer
"lived in Australia and Europe"
Edgar Degas: French impressionist painter; sculptor
Donatello (Donato di Niccolo di Betto Bardi): Italian
sculptor
Anne Ophelia Todd Dowden: American botanical artist,
author, illustrator

Albrecht Durer: German painter, print maker, mathematician

Thomas Eakins: American artist, realism: figures and portraits

Kate Greenaway: British artist, illustrator, author of verse

Paul Grimm: Painter of desert scenes and American Indian portraits

Edith Heath: American ceramicist, founder of Heath Ceramics

Grace Carpenter Hudson: American portrait painter of Pomo Indian children

E.J. Hughes: Canadian artist, painted Canadian landscapes

Frida Kahlo: Mexican painter influenced by indigenous cultures

Amalia Kussner: American artist; miniature portraits of prominent people

Maria Lassnig: Austrian artist, avant-garde human forms

Emanuele Luzzati: Artist, film animator, stage set designer, illustrated children's books

Agnes Martin: American-Canadian artist, abstract expressionist

Piet Mondrian: Dutch painter, founder of the neoplastic movement

Edvard Munch: Norwegian expressionist painter, most famous for *The Scream*

Paul Nash: British painter of war themes and surreal seaside landscapes

Georgia O'Keeffe: American painter

Edward Henry Potthast: American impressionist artist

Nicolas Poussin: French-Italian painter

Qigong a.k.a. Qi Gong: Renowned Chinese calligrapher, artist, painter

Man Ray: American artist, Dada movement

Sir Joshua Reynolds: 18th century English portrait painter

James Rizzi: American pop artist, official artist for 1996 summer Olympics

Theodore Rousseau: French landscape painter

Amalie Seckbach German holocaust artist, painter, sculptress, died in concentration camp

Jean Tabaud: French portrait and landscape artist; ballet dancer

Ralph Thompson: English painter and illustrator of animals

Myrtle Tremblay: American watercolor artist
Leonardo da Vinci: Italian renaissance man: painter, inventor, scientist, anatomist
Andy Warhol: American pop artist icon
Eli Marsden Wilson: English etcher, engraver, painter

Cartoonists who did not sire/bear children

Charles Addams: *The Addams Family*
Ernie Bushmiller: Cartoonist, *Fritzi Ritz*, and the long running *Nancy* comic strip
Edward Gorey: Cartoonist of the macabre, PBS Mystery series
Crockett Johnson (David Johnson Leisk): *Barnaby*
Bill Watterson: *Calvin and Hobbes*
H.T. Webster: Political cartoonist, *The Timid Soul*, character Caspar Milquetoast
Note: Dr. Seuss had no biological children but had stepchildren from his 2nd wife's first marriage.

Champion Athletes who did not sire/bear children:

Edwin Yancey (a.k.a. Yancy) Argo (American) Member of first U.S. Olympic team to win gold medal in equestrian events
Dan Bain (Canadian) Ice hockey Hall of Fame 1949, figure skating, gymnastics, cycling championships
Olav Olavson Bjaaland (Norwegian) Champion skier: Holmenkollen medal; and explorer with first group to reach South Pole
Harry E. Cooper: World Golf Hall of Fame, numerous championships
Jim Corbett (American) World heavyweight boxing champion, actor
Gertrude Ederle: First woman to swim the English Channel; Olympic gold medal 1924
Althea Gibson (American) Tennis champion, first black woman to win at Wimbledon
Chandler Harper (American) Winner of 7 Professional Golf Tournaments
Sonja Henie (Norwegian) Olympic Gold Medal figure skater; movie actress

Eleanor Holm (American) Olympic swimmer, gold medalist 1932

Duke Kahanamoku (American) Olympic swimmer, 3 gold medals, 2 silver, 1912, 1920, 1924

Bobby Kerr (Irish-Canadian) Olympic Gold Medal sprinter, 1908

Billie Jean King (American) Tennis; numerous championships, Associated Press Female Athlete of the Year, 1967

Viola Cady Krahn (American) Hall of Fame diving champion, 17 world titles, lived to be 102

Bob Maitland (British) Olympic silver medalist in cycling 1948; world champion in 65–69 age category 1989

Lia Manoliu (Romanian) 1968 Olympic gold medalist, discus thrower; participated in 6 Olympics

Helen Wills Moody (American) Tennis Int'l Hall of Fame, Olympic gold medalist

Annie Oakley (American) Legendary sharpshooter

Maureen Orcutt (American) Golf champion, two USGA championships, won more than 65 major tournaments

Louis Rubenstein (Canadian) North America's first world figure-skating champion

Max Schmeling: (Germany) World heavyweight boxing champion

Helen Stephens: (American) Olympic sprinter, 2 gold medals 1936

Richard Verderber: (Austrian) Fencing, silver medal, 1912 Olympics; national championships in sabre and foil fencing

Stanley "Stan" Wagner (Canadian) Olympic gold medal, ice hockey 1932

Grete Waitz (Norwegian) Marathon runner, Olympics silver medal, World Championships gold medal, won nine NYC Marathons,

Willye White (American) Olympic silver medalist in track and field

Katarina Witt: (German) Figure skater, 2 Olympic gold medals, 5 world championships

Mildred 'Babe' Didrikson Zaharias (American) Olympic Gold medalist in track and field

Emil Zatopek (Czechoslovakian) Olympic gold medal runner, broke 18 world records

Note: This category of Champion Athletes did not include research on members of commercial team sports: football, basketball and baseball. And in searching for child-free Olympic medalists, it became readily apparent that there is little conflict of interest between competing in these games and parenting, as these athletes tend to be young and childless during their competitive years and still have plenty of time for families after their Olympic glory days are over. For instance, Romanian gymnast Nadia Comaneci was a mere fourteen (and again eighteen) years of age when she won medals in the 1976 and 1980 Olympics. At age thirty-three she married gold medal gymnast Bart Conner, and Nadia became a mother in 2006 when she was forty-four. [1]

Comedians who did not sire/bear children:

Imogene Coca: TV comedienne
Benny Hill: Comedian, British TV
Jay Leno: TV monologues
Steve Martin: Comic actor
Minnie Pearl (a.k.a. Sarah Colley): Comedienne
Gilda Radner: TV comedienne, *Saturday Night Live*

Dancers/Choreographers who did not sire/bear children:

Alvin Ailey: American choreographer, founded Alvin Ailey
American Dance Theatre
George Balanchine: American choreographer, founded NYC
Ballet
Maurice Béjart: Choreographer, Europe
Svetlana Beriosova, Ballerina, London Royal Ballet
Natalia Bessmertnova: Ballerina, Bolshoi Ballet
Edouard Borovansky: Ballet director, Borovansky Ballet,
Australia
Erik Bruhn: International ballet star
Janet Collins: First principle black ballet dancer at Metropolitan Opera; broke ballet color line
Alexandra Danilova: Russian-American ballerina
Felia Doubrovska: Balanchine ballerina
Suzanne Farrell: Ballerina NYC Ballet

---

1 Wikipedia http://en.wikipedia.org/wiki/Nadia_Com%C4%83neci

Celia Franca: British ballet soloist; founded National Ballet of Canada

Alexander Godunov: Russian Bolshoi and American Ballet Theatre

Martha Graham: Modern ballet dancer-choreographer, pioneered modern ballet

Lucile Grahn: Ballerina of the Romantic period

Judith Jamison: Alvin Ailey Dance Co., principle dancer, company director

Robert Joffrey: Dancer Choreographer, Joffrey Ballet Company

Anatol Joukowsky: Dancer, choreographer, folk ballet

Nora Kaye: Ballerina, American Ballet Theatre

Eleanor King: Modern ballet dancer, Humphrey-Weidman Company

Pauline Koner: Dancer; choreographer, modern ballet

Olga Lepeshinskaya: Prima Ballerina, Bolshoi Ballet

Alicia Markova: British ballerina

Ekaterina Maximova: Russian Ballerina, Bolshoi Ballet

Lola Montes: Flamenco dancer

Nadia Nerina: Ballerina with London Royal Ballet

Rudolph Nureyev: Internationally acclaimed ballet dancer

Ruth Page, Dancer-choreographer, founded Chicago Opera Ballet

Anna Pavlova: Russian ballerina

Maya Plisetskaya: Russian ballerina

Jerome Robbins: Choreographer: American Ballet Theatre, NYC Ballet, Broadway

Ginger Rogers: Famous Hollywood dance team: Fred Astaire and Ginger Rogers

Josephine Schwartz: Choreographer, founder of Dayton Ballet Co.

Ted Shawn: Modern ballet dancer-choreographer

Zachary Solov: Ballet dancer; choreographer for the Metropolitan Opera

Phyllis Spira: South Africa's prima ballerina; also London Royal Ballet

Ruth St. Denis: Modern ballet dancer and choreographer

June Taylor: Choreographer, June Taylor Dancers, Jackie Gleason Show

Glen Tetley: Dancer-choreographer of modern and classical ballet

Tamara Toumanova: Russian-born American Ballerina
Galina Ulanova: Russian prima ballerina
Ninette de Valois: Founder of London Royal Ballet
Sallie Wilson: Principal ballet dancer American Ballet
Theatre
Berta Yampolsky: Co-founder and artistic director of Israel
Ballet Company

Fashion Designers who did not sire/bear children:

Giorgio Armani: Fashion designer
Coco Chanel: Fashion designer, and perfumes
Christian Dior: Fashion designer
Jean Muir: English fashion designer

Film makers/directors who did not sire/bear children:

Michelangelo Antonioni: Italian filmmaker, Oscar for life-
time achievement
George Cukor: American film Director
Danièle Huillet: French film maker
Ismail Merchant: Film producer, director from India

Food-related personalities who did not sire/bear children:

Dr. Robert Atkins: Diet guru
James A. Beard: Renowned chef, TV and books
Julia Child: Renowned chef, TV and books

Founders who did not sire/bear children:

Clarissa "Clara" Barton: Founded the American Red Cross
Charles Joseph Bonaparte: US Atty-General under Teddy
Roosevelt; founded FBI
Salvatore Capezio: Famous shoemaker; founder of Capezio
ballet shoes
Jim E. Casey: Founded United Parcel Service
Carrie Chapman Catt: Founder of League of Women Voters
Eugene Victor Debs: Union organizer, founded Int'l Work-
ers of the World
Hans Fantel: Founding editor of Stereo Review; columnist
for NY Times
Stephen Girard: Philanthropist, founder of Girard College

Hermann Gmeiner: Founder of SOS Children's Villages for
orphaned children

Milton S. Hershey: Famous candy maker; founder of Hershey Chocolate Company

Johns Hopkins: Founder of Johns Hopkins University and
Hospital

Anna Jarvis: Founded Mother's Day Holiday, but regretted
its commercialism

Juliette Gordon Low: Founder of the Girl Scouts of America

Alice Stokes Paul: Suffragist who founded National Wom-
en's Party

William Barton Rogers: Founder of Massachusetts Institute
of Technology

Chris R. Tame: Founder and president of Libertarian
Alliance

Raffaele Tudisco: Founder/Amici Opera Co.

Historians who did not sire/bear children:

Mary Boykin Miller Chesnut: Civil War diary; honored on
US postage stamp

Elizabeth Ellet: 19th century historian, *The Women of the
American Revolution*, 3 volumes

Samuel Pepys: Historian, naval administrator

Ida M. Tarbell: American historian, journalist, muckraker

Alexis de Tocqueville: 19th century French political philosopher, historian, noted for *Democracy in America*

Inventors who did not sire/bear children:

Robert Adler: Physicist for Zenith, co-inventor of TV re-
mote control

Alfred Mosher Butts: Architect and inventor of the Scrabble
game

George Washington Carver: Inventor, scientist, invented
hundreds of uses for peanuts

George Eastman: (Eastman-Kodak) revolutionized
photography

George Washington Gale Ferris: Invented the Ferris wheel

Robert H. Goddard: Early rocket scientist, invented first
liquid propelled rocket

Andrew Smith Hallidie: Mechanical genius, invented the
cable car

Felix Hoffmann: Chemist, Invented aspirin
David Edward Hughes: Invented telegraph printer and
microphone
Elijah McCoy: African American inventor, over 50 patents
"The real McCoy"
James Nasmyth: Invented steam hammer and other indus-
trial tools
Freelan Oscar Stanley: Inventor of the steam-powered
automobile
Nikola Tesla: Electrical genius who invented the alternating
current, and wireless radio
Leonardo da Vinci: Artist/inventor, advanced civil engineer-
ing, optics, hydrodynamics
Felix Wankel: Invented the rotary engine
Orville Wright: Invented the airplane
Wilbur Wright: Invented the airplane
Katherine Wright: "The third Wright Brother"
(see also Scientists, below)

Journalists, news reporters, editors who did not sire/bear
children:

Jules Francois Archibald: Australian journalist
Nellie Bly (a.k.a. Elizabeth Cochrane): Extraordinary jour-
nalist, adventurer
Margaret Bourke-White: Famous photo-journalist, Life
Magazine
Ed Bradley: TV news journalist, CBS News, 60 Minutes
Dorothy Dix: Pioneer advice columnist; newspaper editor
Oriana Fallaci: International journalist
John Fox Jr.: Journalist (19th century), New York Sun and New
York Times, novelist
Molly Ivins: Political columnist
Robert McCormick: Publisher of Chicago Tribune
Carlos Monsivais: Mexican author, journalist, leading intel-
lectual, won over 33 awards
Ethel Payne: American Journalist "First Lady of the Black
Press"
Jessica Savage: Television broadcaster and news reporter
Diane Sawyer: Television journalist, newswoman, political
correspondent,

Margaret 'Lionel' Shriver: *Journalist, novelist, Wall Street Journal, Financial Times, The New York Times, The Economist*

Joan Smith: English novelist and journalist

Gloria Steinem: Journalist; editor, *Ms. Magazine*

Ida M. Tarbell: American journalist, muckraker who investigated Standard Oil Co.

Ernest Lawrence Thayer: Columnist/*San Francisco Examiner*, best known for poem, *Casey at the Bat*

Dorothy Townsend: First woman to cover local news for *LA Times*, 1966 Pulitzer Prize for coverage of Watts riots

Judges who did not sire/bear children:

Benjamin N. Cardozo: U.S. Supreme Court Justice, 1932 until his death

Abe Fortas: US Supreme Court Justice

Elena Kagan: U.S. Supreme Court Justice

Burnita Shelton Matthews: First woman judge appointed to a Federal District Court

Sonia Sotomayor: U.S. Supreme Court Justice

Lyricists who did not sire/bear children:

Ray Evans: Hollywood lyricist, songs include *Mona Lisa, Silver Bells*

William Gilbert: lyricist, librettist, dramatist, Gilbert and Sullivan

Ira Gershwin: Lyricist with brother, George Gershwin, and other composers

Mathematicians who did not sire/bear children:

Maria Gaetana Agnesi: Mathematician; author of *Analytical Institutions*

Antoine Deparcieux: French mathematician

Kurt Godel: Mathematician, logician, philosopher

Joseph Lagrange: Mathematician and astronomer

Andrei Nikolaevich Kolmogorov: Foremost 20th century Soviet mathematician

Emmy Noether: Prominent mathematician

Blaise Pascal: Mathematician, physicist

William Tutte: Mathematician and cryptographer, cracked German code WWII

Music, classical musicians who did not sire/bear children:

Gertrude Foster Brown: Suffragist, pianist with the Philharmonic in Berlin

Lady Evelyn (Rothwell) Barbirolli: Oboe soloist, London Royal Symphony and U.S.

Imogen Cooper: Concert pianist

Norman Vilsack Frauenheim: Internationally acclaimed pianist

Helen Gaskell: Oboist with the BBC Symphony Orchestra

Percy Grainger: Pianist, saxophone player, composer

Laura Archera Huxley: Writer, concert violinist (musical prodigy)

Czeslaw Marek: Polish concert pianist and composer of chamber music

John Marston: lead harpist, BBC and London Symphonies, and for Sinatra and Beatles

Dorothy Stone: Virtuoso flutist, composer

Guilhermina Suggia: Celebrated cellist

Shinichi Suzuki: Violinist, taught thousands of young children to play violin, "Suzuki method"

Magdalena Tagliaferro: Critically acclaimed classical pianist, played into her nineties

Mitsuko Uchida: Internationally acclaimed classical pianist

Pablo Casals: World famous cellist

Eugene George Istomin: Pianist, protégé of Pablo Casals

Fritz Kreisler: Violinist, composer

Percy Grainger: Pianist, saxophone player, composer

Dorothy Stone: Virtuoso flutist, composer

Franciszek Zachara: Pianist, composer

(See "composers" and "conductors" for more names of classical musicians)

Music, composers who did not sire/bear children:

Maria Teresa d'Agnesi (Italian) classical dramatic works, sonatas, music for harpsichord

Mily Balakirev (Russian) classical composer, conductor

Samuel Barber (American) modern classical music, opera, choral, orchestral, piano

Amy Beach (American) classical music

Ludwig van Beethoven (German) classical and romantic periods

Vincenzo Bellini (Italian) opera composer

Irénée Marius Bergé: (French- American.) Composed classical suites, choral cantatas, music for silent films

Hildegard von Bingen a.k.a. St. Hildegard of Bingen: (German) Liturgical songs and poems

Marc Blitzstein (American) Theatre composer. *The Cradle
Will Rock*

Johannes Brahms (German) Romantic period of classical
music

Benjamin Britten (English) operas, symphonies, sonatas,
concertos

Anton Bruckner (Austrian) symphonies, choral music

Revol Samoilovich Bunin (Russian) Symphonies, sonatas

John Cage (American) avant garde

Frederic Chopin (French) Romanticism, piano solos

Aaron Copland (American) ballets, symphonies, film music

Arcangelo Corelli (Italian) Baroque period

Manuel de Falla (Spanish) opera, choral, orchestral, piano
music

Frederick Delius (English) orchestral, chamber music, concertos, operas,

Josquin Des Pres (Franco-Flemish) Renaissance

George Gershwin (American) classical, popular and
jazz, *Rhapsody in Blue*

Vittorio Giannini: (American) Neo-romantic, operas, art
songs, symphonies, choral works

Mikhail Glinka (Russian) Classical

Christoph Willibald Gluck (German-Austrian) operas of
early classical period

George Frideric Handel (German-English) Baroque period

Joseph Hayden (Austrian) symphonies, string quartets,
piano trios, concertos, masses

Paul Hindemith (German) opera, orchestral, concert, chamber, vocal

Ruggiero Leoncavallo (Italy) opera composer

George Lloyd (English) late Romantic-classical period

Frederick Loewe (Austrian-American) Musical theatre
composer, *Gigi, My Fair Lady, Camelot, Brigadoon*

Modest Mussorgsky (Russian) Romantic period

Buxton Orr (Scottish) songs, chamber and orchestral music, films

Giovanni Battista Pergolesi (Italian) Comic opera

Cole Porter (American) songwriter, popular song classics, Broadway

Maurice Ravel (French) Impressionist music, *Bolero*

Ottorino Respighi (Italian) opera, symphonic poems

Sigmund Romberg (Hungarian-American) operettas

Gioacchino Rossini (Italian) opera

Erik Satie (French) "eccentric impressionist"

Will Schaefer: Composer of TV music; *I Dream of Jeannie, Flintstones*, Pulitzer Prize for concert piece *The Sound of America*

Franz Schubert (Austrian) symphonies, operas, piano music

Dame Ethel Smyth (English) choral music, symphonies and operas

Johann Strauss Jr. (Austrian) "The Waltz King"

Lily Strickland (American) several hundred popular musical works, some performed by orchestra

Arthur Sullivan (British) light opera

Thomas Tallis (English) Composer, organist

Piotr Tchaikovsky (Russian) ballets and symphonies, *Swan Lake, Sleeping Beauty*

Virgil Thomson (American) The American classical music

Johann Baptist Vanhal (Austrian) prolific classical composer

Heitor Villa-Lobos (Brazil) symphonies, operas, ballets, choral music

Antonio Vivaldi (Italian) Baroque period, *The Four Seasons*

William Walton (British) chamber, concerto and vocal music

Roy Web (American) Hollywood film scores

Kurt Weill (German-American) Theatrical, orchestral, *Three Penny Opera*

Johann Baptist Vanhal (Austrian) Classical composer, concertos, symphonies

Ralph Vaughan Williams (British) chamber, choral, opera, orchestra, symphony

Note: A number of other well-known composers were childless, all but briefly: Camille Saint-Saens was a child prodigy who was without children but for a couple years of his life. He married in 1875 and sired two children "who died within six weeks of each other in 1878."[1] Giuseppe Verdi had a son and daughter who both died in infancy; and Edvard Grieg had only one child who died of meningitis at 13 months of age.[2] Gaetano Donizetti had three children, none of whom survived.[3]

Delius may have fathered a child during an affair while in Florida; but even if he did, he never knew the child. Years later he married a woman in Europe, and they had no children.[4]

Music, conductors who did not sire/bear children:

> Howard Barlow: CBS music director; NBC conductor *Voice of Firestone*
> Sir John Barbirolli: NY Philharmonic and Hallé Orchestras
> Howard Harold Hanson: Composer, conductor, Dir. of Eastman School of Music.
> Andre Kostelanetz: Classical conductor of international acclaim, pops concerts
> Fritz Mahler: Orchestra conductor
> Dimitri Mitropoulos: Orchestra conductor, pianist, composer
> Attilio Poto: Clarinetist, conductor: Metropolitan Opera Company, Boston Symphony
> Argeo Quadri: Opera conductor
> Alberto Zelman: Violinist and conductor

Music, opera singers who did not sire/bear children:

> Emma Abbott (soprano)
> Frances Alda (soprano)
> Marian Anderson (contralto)
> Rose Bampton (soprano)
> Dame Heather Begg (mezzo-soprano)
> Rosina Buckman (soprano)
> Vivian Della Chiesa (soprano)
> Franco Corelli (tenor)

1 Wikipedia http://en.wikipedia.org/wiki/Camille_Saint-Sa%C3%ABns
2 Profiles of Great Classical Composers http://www.52composers.com/index.html
3 Arizona Opera, Learn About Opera http://www.evermore.com/azo/c_bios/donizetti.php3
4 Delius, presentation in Philadelphia (Oct 23, 2005) by Emanuel E. Garcia M.D.: *Devotion, Collaboration and the Salvation of Music* http://thompsonian.info/delius-garcia.html

Regine Crespin (soprano)
Archie Drake (bass-baritone)
Emma Eames (soprano)
Geraldine Farrar (soprano)
Adolph Franosch (bass)
Amelita Galli-Curci (soprano)
Helmet Krebs (tenor)
Lotte Lehmann (soprano)
Frida Leider (soprano)
Adele Leigh (soprano)
Zinka Milanov (soprano)
Grace Moore (soprano)
Inga Nielsen (soprano)
Birgit Nilsson (soprano)
Lillian Nordica (soprano)
Ruth Packer (soprano)
Adelina Patti (soprano)
Marta Perez (mezzo-soprano)
Lily Pons (soprano)
Rosa Ponselle (soprano)
Leontyne Price (soprano)
Nell Rankin (mezzo-soprano)
Manuel Salazar (tenor)
Dame Elisabeth Schwarzkopf (soprano)
Renata Tebaldi (soprano)
May Esther Peterson Thompson (soprano)
Jennie Tourel (soprano)
Raffaele Tudisco: (baritone) Founder/Amici Opera Co., first
    to perform in all 26 Verdi operas
Dame Eva Turner (soprano)
Deon Van der Walt (tenor)
Carol Vaness (soprano)
Astrid Varnay (soprano)
Kyra Vayne (soprano)
Thelma Votipka (mezzo-soprano)
Leonard Warren (baritone)
Camilla Williams: (First Afro-American opera soprano)
Note of interest: It was a much easier task turning up
    names of child-free sopranos than child-free tenors or
    baritones.

Music: Popular singers/musicians who did not sire/bear children:

(Concerts, musical theatre, jazz, soul, gospel, country —
(For opera singers, see above)
Winifred Atwell: International pianist of boogie woogie and ragtime
Gene Autry: Singing cowboy
Mildred Bailey: American jazz singer, honored on US postage stamp
Eubie Blake: Composer, pianist, ragtime and jazz, lived to 100
Del Courtney: Big Band leader, 1930s
Celia Cruz: Cuban-American singer; multiple Grammy winner
Peter Smith Dawson: Baritone singer, concerts; early phonograph recordings
Kenny Gardner: Popular tenor with Guy Lombardo orchestra
Emilio de Gogorza: Baritone singer, classical and popular music concerts
Dobie Gray: Singer, songwriter, soul, country, pop
Albert Wade Hemsworth: Singer-songwriter, guitarist
Billie Holiday: American blues and jazz singer
Mahalia Jackson: Gospel singer; honored on US postage stamp
Frances Langford: Singer, actress, signature song: *I'm in the Mood for Love*
Lotte Lenya: Singer-actress (wife of composer Kurt Weill)
Guy Lombardo: Band leader
Jeanette MacDonald: Singer of light opera; Hollywood film actress
Carmen Miranda: Notable entertainer, North and South America
Henri Mulet: French organist and composer
Dika Newlin: Child prodigy composer; later, music professor and rock performer
Anita O'Day: Singer, big band and jazz
Bernadette Peters: Singer, actress
Travis Reeves: Country singer
Amalia Rodrigues: Popular singing star
Ethel Smith: Organist, "First Lady of the Hammond Organ"

Kate Smith: Popular singer
Fay Templeton: Broadway star, light opera
Sister Rosetta Tharpe: Celebrity gospel singer of the 40s
and 50s
Hank Thompson: Country singing star
Luther Vandross: Grammy winning popular rhythm and
blues singer
Cindy Walker: Country music Hall of Fame songwriter
Ethel Waters: Blues and jazz singer; actress
Mary Lou Williams: Jazz musician and composer

Nobel Prize winners who did not sire/bear children:

Alfred Bernhard Nobel: Established the Nobel Prize for
peace, literature, science, etc.
Jane Addams: Nobel Prize for Peace 1931 US
Vicente Aleixandre: Nobel Prize for Literature 1977 Spain
Ivo Andric: Nobel Prize for Literature 1961 Yugoslavia
Sir Norman Angell: Nobel Prize for Peace 1933 UK
Francis William Aston: Nobel Prize for Chemistry 1922 UK
Emily Greene Balch: Nobel Prize for Peace 1946 US
Samuel Beckett: Nobel Prize for Literature 1969 Ireland
Georg von Bekesy: Nobel Prize for Physiology/Medicine
1961 US
Jacinto Benavente: Nobel Prize for Literature 1922 Spain
Aristide Briand: Nobel Prize for Peace 1926 France
Louis de Broglie: Nobel Prize for Physics 1929 France
James McGill Buchanan: Nobel Prize for Economics 1986
US
Alexis Carrel: Nobel Prize for Physiology/Medicine 1912
France
Robert Cecil: Nobel Prize for Peace 1937 UK
Subrahmanyan Chandrasekhar: Nobel Prize for Physics
1983 US
Donald J. Cram: Nobel Prize for Chemistry 1987 US
Randal Cremer: Nobel Prize for Peace 1903 UK
Peter Henrik Dam: Nobel Prize for Physiology/Medicine
1943, Denmark
Jean Henri Dunant aka Henry Dunant: Nobel Prize for
Peace 1901 Switzerland
Gertrude B. Elion: Nobel Prize for Physiology/Medicine,
1988 US

T.S. Eliot: Poet, Nobel Prize for Literature, 1948 UK
Odysseus Elytis: Nobel Prize for Literature 1979 Greece
Ernest Otto Fischer: Nobel for Chemistry 1973 (West)
    Germany
Hans Fischer: Nobel Prize for Chemistry 1930 Germany
Dennis Gabor: Nobel Prize for Physics 1971 UK
John Galsworthy: Novelist; Nobel Prize for Literature 1932
    UK
Herbert Spencer Gasser: Nobel Prize for Physiology/Medi-
    cine 1944 US
Karl Gjellerup: Nobel Prize for Literature 1917 Denmark
Dag Hammarskjold: Nobel Prize for Peace 1961 Sweden
Arthur Harden: Nobel Prize for Chemistry 1929 UK
Odd Hassel: Nobel Prize for Chemistry 1969 Norway
Verner von Heidenstam: Nobel Prize for Literature 1916
    Sweden
John Richard Hicks: Nobel Prize for Economics 1972 UK
Sir Cyril Norman Hinshelwood: Nobel Prize for Chemistry
    1956 UK
Sir Godfrey Hounsfield: Nobel Prize for Physiology/Medi-
    cine 1979 UK
Cordell Hull: Nobel Price for Peace 1945 US
Frank B. Kellogg: Nobel Prize for Peace 1929 US
Henry W. Kendall: Nobel prize for Physics 1990 US
Sir John Cowdery Kendrew: Nobel Prize for Chemistry
    1962 UK
Imre Kertész: Nobel Prize for Literature 2002 Hungary
Paul R. Krugman: Nobel prize for Economics 2008 US
Selma Lagerlof: Nobel Prize for Literature 1909 Sweden
Dalai Lama: Nobel Prize for Peace 1989 Tibet
Willis Eugene Lamb Jr.: Nobel Prize for Physics 1955 US
Alphonse Laveran: Nobel Prize for Physiology/Medicine
    1907 France
Rita Levi-Montalcini: Nobel Prize for Physiology/Medicine
    1986 Italy
Gabriel Lippmann: Nobel Prize in Physics 1908 France
Andre Michel Lwoff: Nobel Prize for Physiology/Medicine
    1965 France
John James Richard Macleod: Nobel Prize for Physiology/
    Medicine 1923 UK
Maurice Maeterlinck: Nobel Prize for Literature 1911
    Belgium

Barbara McClintock: Nobel Prize for Physiology/Medicine 1983 US

Cesar Milstein: Nobel Prize for Physiology/Medicine 1984 Argentina

Frederic Mistral: Nobel Prize for Literature 1904 France

Gabriela Mistral: Nobel Prize for Literature 1945 Chile

Eugenio Montale: Nobel Prize for Literature 1975 Italy

Stanford Moore: Nobel Prize for Chemistry 1972 US

Vidiadhar Surajprasad Naipaul: Nobel Prize for Literature 2001, Trinidad

Christiane Nüsslein-Volhard, shared Nobel Prize for Physiology/Medicine 1995 Germany

Severo Ochoa: Nobel Prize for Physiology/Medicine 1959 US

Douglas Osheroff: Nobel Prize for Physics 1996, US

Elinor Awan Ostrom: Only woman to win Nobel Prize in Economics 2009 US

Wolfgang Pauli: Nobel Prize for Physics 1945 Austria

Georges Pire a.k.a. Henri Dominique: Nobel Prize for Peace 1958 Belgium

Fritz Pregl: Nobel Prize in Chemistry 1923 Austria

Sully Prudhomme: First Nobel Prize for Literature 1901 France

Wladyslaw Stanislaw Reymont: Nobel Prize for Literature 1924 Poland

Romain Rolland: Nobel Prize for Literature 1915 France

Sir Joseph Rotblat: Nobel Prize for Peace 1995 UK

Leopold Ruzicka: Nobel Prize for Chemistry, 1939 Switzerland

Nelly Sachs: Nobel Prize for Literature, 1966 Sweden

Jean Paul Sartre: Nobel Prize for Literature 1964 France*

Julian Schwinger: Nobel Prize for Physics 1965 US

George Bernard Shaw: Nobel Prize for Literature 1925 Ireland

Hermann Staudinger: Nobel Prize for Chemistry 1953 West Germany

Wisława Szymborska: Nobel Prize for Literature 1996 Poland

Mother Teresa: Nobel Prize for Peace 1979 India

William Vickrey: Nobel Prize for Economics 1996 US

Bertha von Suttner: Nobel Prize for Peace 1905 Austria

Otto Wallach: Nobel Prize for Chemistry 1910 Germany

Otto Warburg, Nobel Prize for Physiology/Medicine 1931
Germany
Patrick White: Nobel Prize for Literature 1973 Australia
Kenneth G. Wilson: Nobel prize for Physics 1982 US
Liu Xiaobo: Nobel Peace Prize 2010 China
Note: *Sartre declined the award

The above names do not comprise a complete list of the Nobel laureates who did not have children; see bibliography for some additional names: Schlessinger, Bernard S. and June H.: *The Who's Who of Nobel Prize Winners* 1901–1990, 2nd ed., Oryx Press, Phoenix AZ 1991. And for a number of Nobel laureates, the Schlessingers state, "Children: No record found." There were a number of years in which the Nobel Prize was not awarded in some categories; and the prize for economics was not issued until 1969.

Notable educators who did not sire/bear children:

Prudence Crandall: Opened first school in Canterbury CT for black girls

Otto Krayer: German pharmacology professor who condemned Hitler's policy

Zelma Watson George: Alternate delegate to U.N., opera singer, speaker, educator

Edith Hamilton: Greek scholar, educator, writer

Dr. Benjamin E. Mays: College president, civil rights leader, SC Hall of Fame

Anne Sullivan: Helen Keller's teacher

Frances E. Willard: Educator, temperance leader, feminist

Philanthropists who did not sire/bear children:

Cecil H. Green: Philanthropist, huge endowments to MIT and other colleges

Grace Groner: Humanitarian, frugal centenarian leaves $7,000,000 to college

Johns Hopkins: Donated money for founding Johns Hopkins University and Hospital

Augustus Juilliard: Philanthropist, Juilliard School of Music

Maude Woods Wodehouse: Philanthropist, left $122 million to various charities d.2003

Philosophers who did not sire/bear children:

Hannah Arendt: (German-American) Political theorist

Francis Bacon (English) Advocated inductive methodology in science and philosophy

Simone de Beauvoir (French) Philosopher on womanhood, The Second Sex

Jeremy Bentham (English) Utilitarianism

Laura Cereta: (Italian) 15th century feminist, taught philosophy, Univ. of Prada

Thomas Hobbes (English) Political philosopher

David Hume, (Scottish) Empiricist

Immanuel Kant (German) Investigation of reason itself, Critique of Pure Reason

Soren Kierkegaard (Danish) Early existentialist

Gottfried Leibniz (German) Rationalism, mathematician

John Locke (English) Early Pragmatist, influenced America's founding fathers

John Stuart Mill (English) Utilitarianism; advocate of women's rights; election reforms

Friedrich Nietzsche (German) Defines human behavior as "the will to power"

Charles Peirce (American) Pragmatist

Plato (Greek) Proponent of forms (archetypes) for defining the cosmos

Ayn Rand (Russian-American) Objectivism

George Santayana (Spanish-American) Naturalism, Pragmatism

Jean-Paul Sartre (French) Existentialist

Baruch Spinoza (Dutch-Portuguese) Rationalism

Emanuel Swedenborg (Sweden) Philosopher, Mystic, the soul-body connection

Thales: Greek philosopher

William Thompson: (Irish) Political philosopher, egalitarian and utilitarian

Ludwig Wittgenstein (Austrian-British) Philosopher of math, logic and language

Pioneering physicians who did not sire/bear children:

Elizabeth Blackwell: First woman physician in the U.S.

Emily Blackwell: Physician

Alice Hamilton: Pioneer doctor in industrial medicine, lived
to 101

Ian Stevenson, M.D., psychiatry professor, investigated
paranormal, reincarnation, Univ. of VA

Dr. Mary Walker: Civil War doctor; advocated reform in
women's fashions

(See Nobel Prize winners for more names of physicians)

Political and world leaders who did not sire/bear children:

James Buchanan: President of the United States

Shirley Chisholm: First black woman elected to Congress

Patricia Roberts Harris: First African American Woman
named to a presidential cabinet

William Pitt: British Prime Minister, 18th Century

Chief Plenty-Coups: Chief of the Crow Nation

James K. Polk: President of the United States

Jeannette Rankin: First U.S. Congresswoman

Condoleezza Rice: US Secretary of State

Margaret Chase Smith: First woman elected to both US
Congress and US Senate

Elizabeth Tudor: Queen Elizabeth I of England

Scientists who did not sire/bear children:

Charles Greeley Abbot: Astrophysicist, devised measurement of solar radiation

William Beebe: Naturalist, oceanographer, ornithologist

Gertrude Bell: Archaeologist

Ruth Benedict: Anthropologist and author

Kristian Olaf Bernhard Birkeland: Physicist; 7 Nobel Prize
nominations

Luther Burbank: Horticulturist, botanist, pioneer in agricultural science

Henry Cavendish: Physicist and chemist, discovered
hydrogen

Nicolaus Copernicus: Astronomer, advanced heliocentric
cosmology

Michael Faraday: English physicist; discovered electromagnetic induction

Sir Charles Frank: Distinguished British physicist

Karl Herzfeld: Physicist known for kinetic theory and
ultrasonics

Admiral Grace Murray Hopper: Pioneer Computer Scientist
Edwin Powell Hubble: Astronomer for whom the Hubble
   telescope is named
Carole Jordan: First woman president of the Royal Astro-
   nomical Society
Joseph Lagrange: Mathematician, astronomer
Marie Paulze Lavoisier: Woman scientist/chemist, coined
   term "oxygen"
Lise Meitner: Physicist, co-discoverer of nuclear fission
Sir Isaac Newton: Astronomer, physicist, advanced theory
   of gravity, laws of motion
Blaise Pascal: Mathematician, physicist
Sir Martin Rees: Astrophysicist, author
Isaac Roberts: Astronomer: awarded Gold Medal of the
   Royal Astronomical Society
Otto H. Schmitt: Biophysicist
James Sherard: Noted botanist, apothecarist
Vandana Shiva: Physicist, ecologist
Otto Struve: Astronomer, proved ionized hydrogen in the
   interstellar medium
Leonardo da Vinci: Designed bridges, machines, buildings,
   canals and forts
   (See above lists of Inventors and Nobel Prize winners
   for more names of scientists)

Social reformers who did not sire/bear children:

(Animal welfare, civil rights, election reform, feminism, etc.)
Jane Addams: Social reformer; Nobel Peace Prize, 1931, US
Susan B. Anthony: Abolitionist, suffragist
Emily Greene Balch: Nobel Peace Prize, 1946, US; a founder
   of the Women's International League for Peace and
   Freedom
Clarissa "Clara" Barton: Founder of American Red Cross;
   feminist
Elizabeth Blackwell: First woman physician in the U.S.
Gertrude Foster Brown: Suffragist, manager of The Woman
   Citizen journal, pianist with the Philharmonic in Berlin
John Cartwright: British reformer who favored American
   independence from England
Margaret Cavendish, Duchess of Newcastle: writer, feminist
Carrie Chapman Catt: Founder of League of Women Voters

Prudence Crandall: Opened first school in Canterbury CT for black girls

Dorothea Dix: Advocate for the poor and mentally handicapped

Gyo Fujikawa: Authored multi-racial children's books before it was politically correct

Emily Greene Balch: Co-founder of Women's Int'l League for Peace and Freedom

Sarah Grimke: Social reformer, feminist, abolitionist, public speaker

Helen Keller: Blind and deaf author and reformer

Vicki Moore: Co-founder of Fight Against Animal Cruelty in Europe

Ralph Nader: Consumer advocate "Public Citizen"

Marcus Nerva: Roman Emperor who enacted humanitarian social reforms

Florence Nightingale: Founder of modern nursing

Alice Stokes Paul: Founded National Women's Party

Rosa Parks: Civil rights activist

Evita (Eva) Perón: First Lady of Argentina and social reformer, "Spiritual Leader of the Nation"

Bernadette Peters: Singer, actress, fund-raiser benefits for animal welfare

Claude Piéplu: French actor; activist for nuclear disarmament

Ernestine Rose: Abolitionist, Suffragist; co-founder of *Association of All Classes, All Nations*

Henry Spira: Founded *Animal Rights International*; got Revlon to stop using animal testing

Gloria Steinem: Feminist spokesperson, editor, *Ms. Magazine*

Bernie Whitebear: Native American leader; founder of *United Indians of All Tribes Foundation*

Safiya Zaghloul: Egyptian pioneer feminist; challenged British occupation

Talk show hosts who did not sire/bear children:

Bob Barker: Long time TV host

Jay Leno: TV Talk show host

Bill Maher: TV host, political satire, *Politically Incorrect*

Yue-Sai Kan: Chinese-American Emmy-winning TV host, entrepreneur, humanitarian

Oprah Winfrey: TV talk show host

Writers who did not sire/bear children:

Forrest J Ackerman: Sci-Fi writer and promoter who coined the term "Sci-Fi"

Zoe Akins: Playwright, screenwriter, 1935 Pulitzer Prize

Louisa May Alcott: Novelist, *Little Women, Little Men*

Hans Christian Andersen: Children's stories

Diana Athill: Literary editor, novelist and memoirist, *Somewhere Towards the End*

Jane Austen: Novelist, *Pride and Prejudice, Sense and Sensibility, Northanger Abbey*

J.M. Barrie: Playwright, and author of Peter Pan

Katherine Lee Bates: Author, poet, wrote Lyrics to *America the Beautiful*

Samuel Beckett: Poet, playwright, *Waiting for Godot*

Roberto Bracco: Dramatist, novelist, nominated for Nobel Prize

Anne Bronte: Novelist, *Agnes Grey*

Emily Bronte: Novelist, *Wuthering Heights*

Helen Gurley Brown: Feminist author, *Sex and the Single Girl*; editor of *Cosmopolitan*

Mikhail Bulgakov: Satirist, novelist, playwright

Octavia Butler: Pioneer black female sci-fi writer

James Cain: Journalist, novelist, crime writer

Lewis Carroll: *Alice's Adventures in Wonderland*

Willa Cather: Novelist, Pulitzer Prize 1923, *One of Ours*

Anton Chekhov: Russian Playwright, *Uncle Vanya, The Seagull*

Arthur C. Clarke: *2001 A Space Odyssey*

Louis Marie-Anne Couperus: Dutch novelist and poet

James Gould Cozzens: Novelist, 1949 Pulitzer Prize, *Guard of Honor*

Mahmoud Darwish : Palestinian poet of many literary prizes

C.J. Dennis: Poetry, prose, children's books of poetry

Kate DiCamillo: Literature for children

Emily Dickinson: American poet

Isak Dinesen: a.k.a. Karen Blixen: Author, *Out of Africa*

Allen Stuart Drury: Novelist, Pulitzer Prize 1960, *Advise and Consent*

George Eliot (a.k.a. Mary Ann Evans)

T.S. Eliot: Poet, editor; Nobel Prize

Edna Ferber: Novelist, playwright, Pulitzer Prize 1925 *So Big*

John Fox Jr.: Journalist, novelist, short story writer

Helen Hamilton Gardener: Writer, suffragist, US Civil Service Commission (1st woman)

Elizabeth George: Novelist

Ellen Glasgow: Novelist, Pulitzer Prize 1942, *In This Our Life*

Frances Goodrich: Playwright, Pulitzer for *Diary of Anne Frank*; Screenwriter, *The Thin Man*, together with her husband Albert Hackett

Albert Hackett: Playwright, Pulitzer for *Diary of Anne Frank*; Screenwriter, *The Thin Man*, together with his wife Frances Goodrich

Thomas Hardy: Novelist, short story writer, poet, *Far From the Madding Crowd*

Anne Hebert: Novelist, poet, playwright

Lillian Hellman: Playwright, The Little Foxes, The Children's Hour

Langston Hughes, African-American poet

Washington Irving: *The Legend of Sleepy Hollow, Rip Van Winkle*

Henry James: American-British short story writer, *The Turn of the Screw*

Sidney Kingsley: Playwright, Pulitzer Prize 1933, Men in White

Antoni Lange: Poet, novelist, philosopher, translator (15 languages) of 19th century literature, Poland

Harper Lee: Novelist: Pulitzer Prize 1961, *To Kill a Mockingbird*

Clive Staples (C.L.) Lewis: Novelist, poet, literary critic, essayist

Howard Phillips (H.P.) Lovecraft: Writer of horror fiction

Joaquim Maria Machado de Assis: Brazilian novelist, short story writer, poet

Katherine Mansfield: short story writer

Colleen McCullough: Novelist, *The Thornbirds*

Henry Louis (H.L.) Mencken: Political correspondent, columnist

James A. Michener: Novelist, Pulitzer Prize 1948 *Tales of the South Pacific*

Edna St. Vincent Millay: First woman to receive Pulitzer Prize for Poetry, 1923

Margaret Mitchell: Novelist, *Gone With the Wind*

Mourning Dove: Native American author, *Cogewea the Half-Blood; Tales of the Okanogans*

Iris Murdoch: Irish-English novelist, *Under the Net, The Unicorn*

Joyce Carol Oates: Novelist, playwright, literary critic

Thomas Paine: *The Rights of Man*

Dorothy Parker: Short story writer, poet

Phoebe Pember: Confederate nurse; published memoirs; honored on US postage stamp

Edgar Allan Poe: Short story writer and poet

Alexander Pope: Poet, translator of Homer

Beatrix Potter: Children's books, *Peter Rabbit*

Ann Radcliffe: Pioneered the Gothic novel, *The Castles of Athlin and Dunbayne*

Marjorie Kinnan Rawlings: Author, Pulitzer Prize 1939, *The Yearling*

George Bernard Shaw: Playwright, *Man and Superman, Pygmalion*

Margaret 'Lionel' Shriver: Novelist, *We Need to Talk About Kevin*

Joan Smith: Novelist and journalist, *What Will Survive*

Thomas Sigismund Stribling: Novelist, Pulitzer Prize 1933 *The Store*

Wislawa Szymborska: Poet, Essayist

Henry David Thoreau: *Walden*

Dale Wasserman: Playwright: *Man of La Mancha*

Edith Wharton, Novelist: Pulitzer Prize 1921, *The Age of Innocence*

Walt Whitman: American poet, *Leaves of Grass*

Thornton Wilder: Playwright, Pulitzer Prize 1938, *Our Town*

Tennessee Williams: Playwright, Pulitzer Prize 1948 & 1955; *Street Car Named Desire*

Virginia Woolf: Novelist, essayist

Marguerite Young: Poetry, fiction and non-fiction, novels (See above lists of Philosophers and Nobel Prize winners for more names of writers.)

Miscellaneous categories of notable people who did not sire/bear children:

MaVynee Betsch: Famous environmentalist known as "Beach Lady"

Jean Dalrymple: American theatrical publicist, producer, playwright, director

Roger Ebert: Film Critic, first film critic to win a Pulitzer Prize

Andre Kertesz: International photographer, pioneered 'distortion techniques

John Maynard Keynes: Economist

Tony Pastor: Father of vaudeville

Robert L. Ripley: Ripley's Believe it or Not

Carol Houck Smith: V.P. and editor-at-large of W.W. Norton & Co. book publisher

Rodney Strong: Broadway dancer and American winemaker

Ganna Walska: Landscape artist "Lotusland"

And here is an interesting category:

Centenarians/Super centenarians who did not bear/sire children:

Charles Greeley Abbot: Astrophysicist, devised measurement of solar radiation; was secretary of Smithsonian Institute; received his last patent at age 101
b. May 31, 1872 Wilton NH
d. Dec 17, 1973 Riverdale MD

Amy Ballinger: Union organizer, nightclub comedienne, Pittsburgh councilwoman, 100
b. Apr 2, 1909 PA
d. Apr 1, 2010 Palm Beach FL

Charlotte Benkner: Named oldest living person, lived to 114
b. Nov 16, 1889 Leipzig, Germany
d. May 14, 2004 North Lima OH

Ruth Bernhard: Pioneer woman photographer; lived to 101
b. 1905 Berlin, Germany
d. Dec 18, 2006 San Francisco CA

Julie Winnefred Bertrand: Named world's oldest woman, lived to be 105
b. Sep 15/16, 1891 Coaticook, Canada
d. Jan 18, 2007 Montreal, Quebec, Canada

Eubie Blake: Composer, pianist, ragtime and jazz, lived to
100
b. Feb 7, 1883 Baltimore MD
d. Feb 12, 1983 Brooklyn NY

Marie Bremont: Lived over 115 years
b. Apr 25, 1886 Noellet, France
d. Jun 6, 2001 Cande (near Paris), France

Russell Alexander Buchanan: WWI & WWII vet, lived to
be 106, still mentally alert
b. Jan 24, 1900 Massachusetts?
d. Dec 6, 2006 Campbridge MA

Patricia Dwinnell Butler: In charge of the U.S. Dept of Justice, library, 101
b. Dec 23, 1907 Brooklyn NY
d. May 27, 2009 La Jolla CA

Laura Carmichael: At her hundredth birthday, living in her
own house, and still active.
b. Nov 20, 1905 Altoona AL
d. Jan 14, 2007 Gainesville FL

Doris Dodman: Celebrated hundredth birthday in good
health; former dancer and model;
b. Feb 2, 1907 Kennington, England[1]

Mary Ellis: Opera singer, stage actress; lived to 105
b. Jun 15, 1897 New York NY
d. Jan 30, 2003 London, England

Alice Hamilton: Pioneer doctor in industrial medicine, lived
to 101
b. Feb 27, 1869 New York NY
d. Sep 22, 1970 Hadlyme CT

---

1 Honored by both the American and British Red Cross for her help with service men
and their families. "When we asked her the secret of her long life, she said she
danced a lot, she never got married and she never had children. She's an extraordinary woman." http://www.thisislocallondon.co.uk/whereilive/tottenham/
display.var.1167623.0.life_is_a_long_song.php (Web site no longer available)

Cecil H. Green: Philanthropist, lived to 102
b. Aug 6, 1900 Manchester, England
d. Apr 11, 2003 La Jolla CA

Grace Groner: Frugal philanthropist leaves $7 million to
college, lived to 100
b. Apr 4, 1909 Lake Co. IL
d. Jan 19, 2010 Lake Forest IL

Ramona Trinidad Iglesias-Jordan: Lived to 114
b. Aug 31, 1889 7:00 AM Utuado, Puerto Rico
d. May 29, 2004 Rio Piedras, San Juan, Puerto Rico

George Johnson: Lived to 112
b. May 1, 1894 Philadelphia PA
d. Aug 30, 2006 Richmond CA

Viola Cady Krahn: Hall of Fame diving champion, 17 world
titles, lived to 102, still active and competing at age 101.
b. 1902 AZ
d. Jun 1, 2004 Orange Co. CA

Mary L. Parr: lived to 113
b. Feb 1, 1889 IN
d. Oct 29, 2002 FL

Emiliano Mercado del Toro: lived to 115
b. 1891 Puerto Rico
d. Jan 24, 2007 Isabela, Puerto Rico

Myrtle Tremblay: Watercolor artist, 102
b. Dec. 9, 1908, Albion, Mich.
d. Sep 3, 1911 New Holland PA

Mrs. Hendrikje 'Hennie' Van Andel-Schipper: World's oldest woman, lived to 115
b. Jun 29, 1890 Smilde, Netherlands
d. Aug 30, 2005 Hoogeveen, Netherlands

Ninette de Valois: Founder, London Royal Ballet, 102
b. Jun 6, 1898 County Wicklow, Ireland
d. Mar 8, 2001 London, England

CHAPTER 6. THE FAMOUS CHILD-FREE: THEIR REASONS FOR
NOT HAVING CHILDREN

Here are some of the reasons that famous people have given for
why they did not have children. And, while the answers are widely
varied, they are all legitimate reasons, for one does not need to jus-
tify not having children. But first, here are comments from two British women who knew adamantly from youth that they did not want
to bear children because of concern for the planet.

From Mail Online, website of the *Daily Mail* British
    newspaper[1]
"Meet the women who won't have babies — because they're
    not eco friendly," by Natasha Courtenay-Smith and
    Morag Turner (2007)

Toni Vernelli:

"Having children is selfish. It's all about maintaining your
genetic line at the expense of the planet," says Toni, 35.

"Every person who is born uses more food, more water,
more land, more fossil fuels, more trees and produces more

---

1   http://www.dailymail.co.uk/femail/article-495495/Meet-women-wont-babies--
     theyre-eco-friendly.html#ixzz1njMZxCwo

rubbish, more pollution, more greenhouse gases, and adds to the problem of over-population." Her husband, Ed, fully agrees.

Sarah Irving and husband Mark Hudson:

"Most young girls dream of marriage and babies. But Sarah dreamed of helping the environment — and as she agonised [sic: British spelling] over the perils of climate change, the loss of animal species and destruction of wilderness, she came to the extraordinary decision never to have a child.

'I realised [British spelling] then that a baby would pollute the planet — and that never having a child was the most environmentally friendly thing I could do.'"

Says Mark, "In short, we do everything we can to reduce our carbon footprint. But all this would be undone if we had a child. . . . Sarah and I don't need children to feel complete. What makes us happy is knowing that we are doing our bit to save our precious planet."

Both couples have had sterilizations.

Reasons famous people have chosen not to have children:

Charles Addams: Cartoonist
In late 1942, he met his first wife, Barbara Jean Day, who purportedly resembled the cartoon character Morticia Addams. The marriage ended eight years later, after Addams, who hated small children, refused to adopt one.
Wikipedia http://en.wikipedia.org/wiki/Charles_Addams

Jane Addams: Social reformer; Nobel Peace Prize winner 1931
"Her parents felt that she had had enough education and were concerned that she would never marry. Jane became despondent. She wanted more in life. If her brothers could have careers in medicine and science, why couldn't she? Besides, she disliked household duties and the prospect of raising children held no appeal."
Women in History, Lincoln Library of Essential Information, Frontier Press Company, 1924
http://lkwdpl.org/wihohio/adda-jan.htm

Diana Athill: Literary Critic, Author
"It surprises her that she's never much minded not having children. 'I love playing with Alexander [a neighbor's child], but I'm glad I'm not his grandmother. Something in me didn't want to get involved in something that was more important than anything else.'"
Interview With Costa Award Winner Diana Athill by Maureen Cleave for the Telegraph.co.uk, January 6, 2009
http://www.telegraph.co.uk/culture/books/4143628/Interview-with-Costa-Award-Winner-Diana-Athill.htmlhttp://www.telegraph.co.uk/culture/books/4143628/Interview-with-Costa-Award-Winner-Diana-Athill.html

Francis Bacon: Philosopher
"He that hath wife and children hath given hostages to fortune; for they are impediments to great enterprises, either of virtue or mischief. Certainly the best works, and of greatest merit for the public, have proceeded from the unmarried or childless men; which both in affection and means have married and endowed the public."
Francis Bacon on Marriage and Single Life posted by Dr. J. http://westerntradition.wordpress.com/2012/04/13/francis-bacon-on-marriage-and-single-life/

Sir John and Lady Evelyn Barbirolli: Classical Music
Sir John, classical conductor; Evelyn, oboe soloist
"The couple never had children because they feared their constant touring would provide an unsettled upbringing."
Announcements.co.uk website on 25th January 2008
http://www.lastingtribute.co.uk/tribute/barbirolli/2722653

Simone de Beauvoir: Author, Philosopher
"Do you think the mothers you know chose to have children? Or were they intimidated into having them? Or, more subtly, were they raised into thinking that it's natural and normal and womanly to have children and therefore chose to have them? But who made that choice inevitable? Those are the values that have to be changed."

Ms. Beauvoir in a 1976 interview by John Gerassi; twenty-five years after the publication of her book, The Second Sex: http://www.marxists.org/reference/subject/ethics/de-beauvoir/1976/interview.htm

Margaret Bourke-White: Celebrated photographer, war correspondent
"She knew herself well enough to choose career over family and never regretted it. '...I needed an inner serenity as a kind of balance. This was something I could not have if I was torn apart for fear of hurting someone every time an assignment of this kind came up...Dashing off at a moment's notice around the globe is wonderful if you are doing the dashing yourself. But if you are the one who stays behind, it must be hard to bear.'"
Janet Worne, "Thoughtful Photography" http://thoughtfulphotography.typepad.com/blog/2009/12/margaret-bourkewhite.html

Laura Cereta: 15th-century Italian feminist, taught philosophy at Univ. of Prada.
"Being childless and widowed in her youth left her ample opportunity to pursue an intellectual course without the burdens of child-rearing and running a household. She was fortunate to have the respectability and social position of one who had married, without the responsibilities of the union."
Answers.com. http://www.answers.com/topic/laura-cereta

Vivian Della Chiesa: Opera singer and TV and radio hostess
"She never had children. 'By choice,' she added. "I didn't think it was right to farm them out. I had to travel so much. Students now fill that void. They are my family,' she said."
Article by Diane Ketcham in NY Times (Aug 3, 1997) http://query.nytimes.com/gst/fullpage.html?res=9B05E7DC1E3AF930A3575BC0A961958260&sec=&spon=&pagewanted=all

Julia Child: Gourmet chef, TV personality, author
Does she regret not having children? A smile graces her face.
"I think it would be nice to be a grandmother. But, no, I don't miss them. I wouldn't have had the career I did if I'd have had children."

Ms. Magazine summer 2003 Live! Eat! Enjoy! Interview by Martha Smilgis
http://www.msmagazine.com/june03/smilgis.asp

Antoine Deparcieux: French mathematician
"Deparcieux never married and had no children, reportedly saying that he simply had no time for it."
Wikipedia http://en.wikipedia.org/wiki/Antoine_Deparcieux

Doris Dodman: Centenarian
"When we asked her the secret of her long life, she said she danced a lot, she never got married and she never had children. She's an extraordinary woman."
Website no longer there.
http://www.thisislocallondon.co.uk/whereilive/tottenham/display.
var.1167623.0.life_is_a_long_song.php

Odysseus Elytis: Poet, essayist, graphic artist, Nobel Prize for Literature 1979
"Elytis never married because he claimed his poetry would suffer, and for the same reason he did not change his lifestyle upon winning the Nobel Prize . . ." [This probably also applied to his philosophy on having children. He did have a girlfriend; however, in the latter years of his life.]
Contemporary Literary Criticism. http://www.enotes.com/
contemporary-literary-criticism/elytis-odysseus

Dame Edith Evans: British stage actress
"Edith never had children and was known to offer the opinion — if queried — that actresses do not perhaps make the most ideal parents."
Edith Evans by Siobhan Staples http://www.retirement-matters.co.uk/
edithevans.htm

Suzanne Farrell: Ballerina
"If I had a child, I'd want to be with it," she explains. "I wouldn't want to give it to somebody else to care for... To have a baby takes at least a year out of a dancer's life, and a year in a dancer's life is a long time."
Dec 1986 Swan's Song http://www.maryellenmark.com/text/maga-
zines/connoisseur/904D-000-002.html

Dag Hammarskjöld: UN Secretary-General 1953–61; Nobel
Prize for Peace 1961
"Hammarskjöld had no wife or family of his own, and
during a press conference he jokingly said that the
UN Charter should contain a clause, which says 'the
Secretary-General of the UN should have an iron consti-
tution and should not be married.'" (Urquhart 1972, p.
25). "Since he had no family, he was able to focus all of
his energy on the UN and work long hours." (Urquhart
1972, p. 26)
*Dag Hammarskjöld by Martin Hagberg, quoting from bio by B. Urqu-
hart, A. Knopf* http://www.daghammarskjold.se/biography/

Albert Wade Hemsworth: Singer-songwriter, guitarist
"His songs were the children he never had; he once said he'd
send them out on their own to see how they'd come
back."
Article by Lorne Browne, Canadian Folk Music Bulletin http://cfmb.
icaap.org/content/36.1/BV36.1art6.pdf

Katharine Hepburn: Actress
"I would have been a terrible mother ... because I'm basically
a very selfish human being. Not that that has stopped
most people from going off and having children."
Biography by Scott Berg, Kate Remembered. http://dir.salon.com/
story/books/review/2003/07/16/kate_bio/index.html?pn=2

Nick Holonyak: Scientist and inventor of the light emitting
diodes (LED)
University of Illinois Professor, inventor of light emitting
diodes (LED) "The couple never had children ('My
graduate students are my children,' he said), and she
[his wife] said he devoted himself to work." *Interview
After Glow* by Dave Evensen https://netfiles.uiuc.edu/hschein/
www/readings/NickHolonyak.pdf

Laura Archera Huxley: Writer, concert violinist (musical
prodigy)
"Asked many years ago why she never had children of her
own, she replied, laughing, 'I never thought I was old
enough to have one.'" And: "Huxley, who never had

children of her own, once described its goal as 'bringing children up loving the world, rather than fearing it as many children do.'"
Obituary, Los Angeles Times, Dec 15, 2007 http://somaweb. org/w/
Laura_Huxley.html
Comment: Ms. Huxley was married to the novelist Aldous Huxley until his death. Even though he had a son from his first marriage, this son was born in 1920 and was in his mid-thirties by the time Laura married Aldous in 1956.

Imre Kertész: Novelist, Nobel Prize for Literature 2002
"Imre Kertész was born in Budapest on November 9, 1929. Of Jewish descent, in 1944 he was deported to Auschwitz and from there to Buchenwald, where he was liberated in 1945. . . . His [novel] *Kaddish* is said for the child he refuses to beget in a world that permitted the existence of Auschwitz."
Nobelprize.org. http://nobelprize.org/nobel_prizes/literature/laureates/2002/kertesz-bio.html

Viola Cady Krahn: Hall of Fame diving champion, 17 world titles, lived to be 102.
"She said she lived such a long life because she was an only child, never had children and ate ice cream every day."
The Washington Post June 5, 2005 obits. http://www.washingtonpost.com/wp-dyn/articles/A17123-2004Jun4.html

Joseph Lagrange: Mathematician and astronomer
"They [Lagrange and wife] had no children, in fact Lagrange had told [Jean Le Rond] d'Alembert [French mathematician] in this letter that he did not wish to have children."
An online biography which cites numerous sources http://www.gapsystem.org/~history/Biographies/Lagrange.html

Maria Lassnig: Austrian artist
"'My mother thought I would be very lucky if I had a husband and became a housewife and mother,' says Lassnig. 'When I was young, I was clever enough to know that if I got married or had children, I would be eaten. I would be sick if I couldn't paint, and I would be schizophrenic

because I would have wanted to do both [paint and have a family]. So I renounced it. I don't understand young women who have a big family and want to make art. I don't think it is possible.'"
Article by Emine Saner, *The Guardian*, June 2008 http://
www.guardian.co.uk/lifeandstyle/2008/jun/18/women.
healthandwellbeing

Bill Maher: TV host, political satire, Politically Incorrect
"When I was 28 years old and a girl said to me, 'Do you like children?' I'd go, 'Well, you know, not right now, but I think someday.' That was a complete lie. I never liked children. I never wanted children, and I was just saying that because I didn't want to lose the fish that was on the end of my hook. I noticed as I got older, I got more honest (because I was able to), and the women were the ones who started to lie to me."
Pittsburgh Post-Gazette, September 18, 2006 article by Patricia Sheridan http://www.post-gazette.com/pg/06261/722702-129.stm

Steve Martin: Comedian
"Asked if he is surprised as to why he has no children, Martin merely smiles. 'I wonder why I don't because they are very, very sweet. Sometimes they're just fascinating and cute even though I know there is the dark side.'"
"Steve Martin's Latest Comedy is Child's Play," Interview by Paul Fischer, Dec 15, 2003
Steve Martin/Cheaper by the Dozen, Interview by Paul Fischer for Film Monthly. http://www.filmmonthly.com/Profiles/Articles/SMartinCheaperDozen/SMartinCheaperDozen.html

Colleen McCullough: Novelist, *The Thornbirds*
"McCullough grew up knowing three things: that she never wanted children, that she loved words and that she would educate herself in the sciences.
And she did: she qualified as a neuroscientist in Sydney before working at Great Ormond Street Hospital in London in the early Sixties."
Article by Robert Gore-Langton, Mail Online (UK) April 5, 2009
http://www.dailymail.co.uk/tvshowbiz/article-1167375/Instant-vomit-The-Thorn-Birds-author-gives-damning-verdict-iconic-TV-series.html

Helen Mirren: Actress
"The Oscar winning actress told an Australian television
   interviewer about a school trip to watch a sex education
   film . . .
Ms. Mirren: 'I went to a single sex convent school, and
   even in Biology classes we weren't taught about sexual
   reproduction. I was about 13, 14, . . . They sat us all
   down, girls and boys, in this horrible school hall . . . this
   film comes on, which is a midwives educational film.
   There is a close-up of a woman having a baby, a close
   up straight up her vagina, and that's all you see, and
   these are thirteen year old boys and girls, and its bloody
   and disgusting. . . . Within thirty seconds two boys had
   fainted and the lights went on and they were carried
   out. . . . I put my hands over my face because I realised
   [sic British spelling] I couldn't watch this. . . . I swear it
   traumatised [sic British spelling] me, I haven't had children and I can't look at anything to do with childbirth,
   it absolutely disgusts me. . . . I think that this film has a
   lot to do with the fact I didn't have children. I'm not a
   motherly sort of person.'"
The Insider http://www.theinsider.com/news/425480_Helen_Mir-
   ren_on_why_she_never_had_children_Childbirth_disgusts_me

Piet Mondrian: Dutch painter, founder of the Neoplastic
   movement
"When asked why he never married, his response was that
   he could not afford being married in his younger years,
   and he never met the right woman in his later years."
The New Netherland Institute Cultural Educational Center
http://www.nnp.org/nni/Publications/Dutch-American/mondrian.html

Stanford Moore: Nobel Prize for Chemistry 1972 US
"Stanford Moore was intensively and single-mindedly
   devoted to science. He consciously avoided activities
   that did not involve science and scientists. This lifelong
   bachelor was an early riser, and he was at his desk or in
   the laboratory throughout the day and on the weekends.
   Yet he was a gracious and hospitable host to his scientific friends and associates." This explains his child-free
   status.

National Academy of Sciences
A Biographical Memoir by Emil L. Smith and C.H.W. Hirs
http://books.nap.edu/html/biomems/smoore.pdf

Edvard Munch: Painter who pioneered Expressionism, best
known for "The Scream"
According to biographer, Sue Prideaux, he referred to his
paintings as his children. "And he never wanted [biolog-
ical] children, as he feared they would become insane."
His art was influenced by hallucinogenic perceptions
and by visions.
Edvard Munch: Behind the Scream by Sue Prideaux http://www.
hoover.org/publications/policyreview/2913276.html

Ralph Nader: Consumer advocate, Public Citizen, author
"Nader is well known for his modest lifestyle. He lives alone
in a Washington apartment and does not own a car. He
never married and has no children. He told The New
York Times in 1995 that he didn't want to be an absentee father or husband. 'That would have been terrible,'
he said."
Web page no longer available http://www.cnn.com/LECTION/2004/
special/president/candidates/nader.html
"He never married or had children because he didn't want
to be 'an absentee father.' Then again, he gets to spend
all of his waking hours doing what he loves best: writing books, dogging multinational corporations and nag-
ging Congress."
Los Angeles Times, Faye Fiore Times staff writer, June 18,
2000 http://articles.latimes.com/2000/jun/18/news/mn-42246

Vidiadhar Surajprasad Naipaul: Novelist, Nobel Prize for
Literature 2001
"Naipaul has never had children, whom he has said 'would
have come between me and the work' He has also said: 'I
love privacy. I couldn't bear the idea of having children.
I don't want a crowd,' a view which he once ascribed to
having grown up in the claustrophobia of an extended
family."
The Guardian UK, Sep 8, 2001 by Maya Jaggi http://www.
guardian.co.uk/education/2001/sep/08/artsandhumanities.
highereducation

James Nasmyth: Engineer, inventor
"It was a cosy little cottage at Patricroft. We had named
it 'Fireside.' It was small, but suitable for our requirements. We never needed to enlarge it, for we had no
children to accommodate."
James Nasmyth, Engineer, *An Autobiography*, edited by Samuel Smiles L.L.D., Chapter XX p.375 *Leaving Fireside* http://
books.google.com/books?
http://www.familytreelegends.com/records/47175?c=read&page=404

Dika Newlin: Child Prodigy, composer, professor
Never married, "Newlin, 79, never wanted children—'not
having known them, I can't deal with them'—but students find her forever hip."
People Magazine Feb 17, 2003, *Prodigies Grow Up*, by Richard
Jerome, Christina Cheakalos, Susan Horsburgh http://
www.people.com/people/archive/article/0,,20139308,00.html

Rudolph Nureyev: Ballet star
On why he didn't want children: "What if they were not as
good as me? What would I do with those imbeciles?"
IMDB bio http://www.imdb. com/name/nm0638159/bio

Dr. Christiane Nusslein-Volhard: 1995 Nobel Prize
for Physiology/Medicine
"In German science, we have a special problem. We lose
talented women at the time they get pregnant. Some
of it occurs because they are encouraged — by their
husbands, bosses and the government — to take long
maternity leaves. Germanic thinking has it that children
can only be properly brought up if the actual mother is
cleaning and picking up. Many stop their research for
two or three years. Later, these young women find it
difficult to get back. They drop out."
New York Times, interview by Claudia Dreifus, Jul 4, 2006
http://www.nytimes.com/2006/07/04/science/04conv.html

Anita O'Day: Jazz singer
"She said she never wanted children, telling *People magazine*,
'Ethel Kennedy dropped 11. There are enough people in
the world. I did my part by raising dogs.'"

SWINGMUSIC.net http://www.swingmusic.net/Anita_ODay.html

Michelle Paver: Novelist, children's books
"A natural loner, she is happy to be without husband or
   children and has made no changes to her life apart from
   increasingly adventurous travel to the remaining wild
   places of the world. . . . Unencumbered by children or
   the desire for Armani clothes, she is free to explore all
   her childhood fantasies."
Wolf Sister: An interview with Michelle Paver by Amanda Craig
   http://amandacraig.com/pages/childrens/articles/michelle_paver_
   interview.htm

Guy Pearce: Australian actor
Actor Guy Pearce has revealed that he and his wife of 11
   years — Kate Mestitz — don't plan on ever having
   children. "I think there are way too many people in the
   world anyway, so Kate and I are doing our bit and not
   having any," the Time Machine star said.
Guy added to his explanation in the latest issue of GQ
   Magazine, telling the interviewer that while he likes
   kids, he believes fatherhood would be about as fun as
   breaking a leg.
   http://www.staralicious.com.au/guy-pearce-i-dont-want-children/
Has he changed his mind about not having children? "I
   don't want to have kids for a number of reasons,"
   he says. "I don't think I'd be emotionally consistent
   enough. I know that having a child is the ultimate in
   creation, but I already have so much creativity in my life,
   there's no space left. A friend of mine said, 'Oh, but you
   learn so much about yourself by having children.' Well,
   that's what my therapist is for." The couple's three dogs,
   he adds, provide more than enough for him to dote on.
The Australian Magazine, Oct 29, 2011, Greg Callahan
   http://www.theaustralian.com.au/news/features/talk-of-the-town/
   story-e6frg8h6-1226176181405

Ayn Rand: Novelist, philosopher
"Rand herself had no children, claiming she need all her
   time and energy to work."

"Objectivism and Families" *Understanding the Obligations Between Parent and Child* http://obsequiosity.home.Marsi.com/ philosophy/children.html

Martin Rees: Astrophysicist, author
"In a sense because I've never been athletic and because I've never had children that probably means I'm less orient-ed age-wise than some people. I'm 60 but I don't really feel any different from when I was 30."
The Guardian, Apr 24, 2003, Simon Hattenstone
http://www.guardian.co.uk/life/interview/story/0,12982,941906,00.html

Elisabeth Schwarzkopf: Opera soprano
"Miss Schwarzkopf leaves no immediate survivors. Asked once whether she regretted having had no children, she replied, 'I have 500 children, the songs I sing.'"
New York Times Aug 4, 2006, Anthony Tommasini http://www.nytimes.com/2006/08/04/arts/music/04schwarzkopf.html?pagewanted=all

Maurice Sendak: Author and illustrator of children's books
"I taught for a long time in New York, and I love teach-ing. I love having young people around. I've never had children; I'm never going to have children. The students became my ersatz kids. Watching them, criticizing them and loving them, they become my family."
"Maurice Sendak: A Portrait of the Illustrator for Children As a Middle-Aged Man" interview by Hank Nuwer
http://www.hanknuwer.com/sendak.html

Margaret 'Lionel' Shriver: Author, *We Need to Talk About Kevin*
She decided when she was eight that she didn't want to have children.
"Novelist Lionel Shriver has been queasy about the prospect of having children since she was a child herself. By her early forties, with little time remaining before the bio-logical clock struck twelve, Ms. Shriver decided to con-front what she most feared. What could be worse than having a baby, and then concluding that you'd made a mistake, when it was too late?"

Reading Groups Guide, interview http://www.readinggroupguides.
com/guides3/we_need_talk_kevin2.asp#essay

Australian Broadcasting Corporation, Author Shriver
speaks about writing, motherhood, Reporter: Kerry
O'Brien, 12/09/2006

http://www.abc.net.au/7.30/content/2006/s1739456.htm

Joan Smith: Novelist

"The cultural pressure to have children is absolutely enor-
mous. Both men and women often seem very threatened
by my choice, . . . Someone once even suggested to me
that I should pretend to look sad about it when I was
asked why I didn't have children! . . . Childbirth is still
seen as the defining act of female identity. Childless but
sexually active women carry the stigma of having refused to undertake the defining act of female sacrifice."

"Women Who Don't Want Children" by journalist Rose-
mary Bailey, *Vogue Magazine 1995*

http://www.rosemarybailey.com/?page_id=248

Holland Taylor: Actress, films and theatre

From a Hollywood reunion for actors who played mothers
and children:

"As in reality, not all TV moms are good ones, especially
Taylor's bawdy Evelyn Harper on 'Two and a Half
Men.'"

According to Ms. Taylor, "I think what has trained me and
prepared me for this role, as this particular mother, is
that I have never had children. And not only have I never had children, but I didn't even notice that I haven't
had children. So, with that in mind, I am beautifully
equipped to play Evelyn Harper."

"A mother and child reunion for TV actors", Associated
Press, May 8, 2008

"On-screen children honor their make-believe mothers at
Academy event"

http://www.accesshollywood.com/_article_9411

Mitsuko Uchida: Internationally acclaimed classical pianist

According to *Biography Today*, "She has never married and
has never had children, believing that her career would
not have been possible if she had had a child. Because of

the travel required, as well as preparation, both children and her work would have suffered greatly. She enjoys other activities such as reading and theater, and has little time for much else other than music; and it is a positive choice that Uchida has made. As she told Catherine Pate in an interview, 'I have no other passions. I like other things, but I only have enough room for one real passion, and that is music.' "

Oxford Grove Music Encyclopedia http://www.answers.com/topic/mitsuko-uchida

Carol Vaness: International opera singer
"I'm actually pretty normal for a soprano! But I'm really, really dedicated to music. That's why I didn't have children: I can't do anything half-assed. My natural instinct is to give 180 percent, but then you've spent it all, and I need to save myself."

"Soprano takes on two demanding roles," by Melinda Bargreen, Music critic for *Seattle Times* http://seattletimes.nwsource.com/html/entertainment/2002143195_opera09.html

Christopher Walken: Actor
"Walken has stated in interviews that not having children is one of the reasons he has had such a prolific career."

Wikipedia http://en.wikipedia.org/wiki/Christopher_Walken#Personal_life

Mae West: Actress, comedienne
On children: "I knew I didn't want children. When I was a little girl, I wanted a doll. But I knew that a doll wasn't a baby. You can just put your dolly away when you don't feel like playing that game anymore. But I don't think I was meant to be a mother. I don't think a woman should have a baby unless she's prepared to love that baby more than she loves herself."

Mae West: Deep in the Heart, Mae West website March 31, 2009 http://maewest.blogspot.com/2009_03_01_archive.html

Berta Yampolsky: Co-founder and artistic director of Israel Ballet Company

Berta Yampolsky and Hillel Markman (husband and wife) are the artistic directors of Israel's only classical ballet company.

In an interview with Naana Lansky, Ms. Yampolsky has this to say about children: "I have the best husband in the world. Children are love and happiness, but children are also very difficult. The moment you have children you've finished with your life. You're no longer worth anything. Everything revolves around the children. It's impossible to divide your life between art and children. A child is not a dog. We had a problem with the Israeli dancers who became mothers. Suddenly she has to leave early, her child is sick, she has fever. That's impossible."

Mr. Markman adds the following comments: "Because we started to dance relatively late," explains Markman, "had we decided to bring children into the world that would have forced us to stop our career and we couldn't do that. Anyone can be a mother, but not everyone can be a ballerina, and I, as opposed to Berta, am not sorry that we have no children. Even raising dogs is a difficult task."

Strictly come dancing by Naana Lanski, Haaretz Jan 18, 2007
Strictly come dancing, by Naana Lanski www.haifa-israel.info/yampolsky.doc

CHAPTER 7. MORAL CONSIDERATIONS FOR NOT HAVING CHILDREN

The world human population in 1900 was estimated at 1.6 billion people. In 1999 it reached 6 billion. In March 2014, it was appraoching 7,300,000,000.[1] Most of the human population growth has occurred within just the past century. It is still growing.

What is your reaction to these statements? What are you thinking? Some people are not that concerned about these numbers, and trust that mankind will solve the problems caused by population growth. These individuals need to ask themselves why, then, has mankind not done so already. Our technology keeps advancing, yet it has failed to keep pace with population growth. But why on earth do we still have population growth? Who is to blame? Is humanity this apathetic to the problems which it creates?

So many of earth's problems are man-made and have well-known solutions. Why then does humanity insist on living with the problems? Is there such a vast lack of intelligence? Or is it a vast lack of morals? Could it be that many people just don't care that much about world problems as long as they, personally, are doing all right? These would be people who lack a global consciousness.

1 Worldometers http://www.worldometers.info/world-population/

Could it also be that part of the population just doesn't really care that much about world problems because of religious conditioning that focuses on an 'after-life' to the detriment of life here on earth? Many religious fanatics have been conditioned to believe that they are the 'chosen ones' and thus eagerly await Armageddon. They believe that when things get really bad here on earth that they will be lifted into a safe place. Well guess what? Things are already really bad here on earth; and their type of immature thinking fosters the very bigotry that will surely make Armageddon a self-fulfilling prophesy.

While religious fanatics are waiting around for their much desired Armageddon, they should not be allowed to drag the whole world down with them. To believe that one belongs to a selected class of humans who are the 'chosen ones' is self-centeredness. Those who await and welcome an Armageddon are definitely advocating such self-centeredness. They see themselves as being superior to others not of their beliefs: others not like themselves. This is a sign of stunted moral development. So it's not surprising that people of this mind-set tend to oppose birth control. They adhere to the biblical philosophy: be fruitful and multiply. After all, that will surely speed Armageddon on its way.

Religion and morality are often at odds with one another, and overpopulation is a case in point. While organized religions are preoccupied with a hypothetical hereafter, morality is based on the here and now. This is not to say that there is no hereafter. There may also be a here before; however, morality is based upon neither. Moral correctness is judged by a person's behavior as pertaining to life here on earth.

We do not hold non-human animals or small children morally responsible for their actions, which they are unable to comprehend. Likewise, if there is intelligence higher than our human species then that intelligence cannot hold us morally accountable for that which we are unable to comprehend. Once again, moral considerations must be based on the tangible world in which we live. If there is life preceding or following our time here on earth, this is a matter for speculation, hypothesis, religion, metaphysics, but not to be confused with moral issues, which pertain only to life here on Earth, period! As for all the rest? It is certainly something to explore, to occupy our thoughts, but must not be confused with morality.

What is moral is what works best for life on this planet, what brings the greatest good and the least suffering to all mankind. And there's no need to stop with mankind; we are not the only species capable of experiencing pain. This greatest good/least suffering philosophy is known as utilitarianism, and one of its greatest exponents was the philosopher, John Stuart Mill. And as an animal rights advocate, he also expressed concern about the wellbeing and/or suffering of other sentient beings.

The utilitarian principle should not be confused with egoistic hedonism — the philosophy that self-pleasure is the greatest good. Obviously, if the drive for self-pleasure were the highest attainment in life, we would incessantly run into conflicts of interest with other people. An individual's pursuit of self-pleasure would find itself in constant collision with that of other individuals' drive for self-pleasure.

So what does all this have to do with procreation? Couples choose to procreate to fulfill their own self-interests. And it is a self-interest that, unregulated, is in conflict with the 'greatest good' principle because overpopulation has lowered the quality of life for mankind and for life on this planet as a whole. Just because people are physically capable of procreation does not establish, *a priori* that it is moral to procreate. People are physically capable of all sorts of acts that are hardly moral.

Over-consumption is gluttony but over-procreation is also gluttony, and ironically it is a form of gluttony expressed by impoverished people who can least afford it. But in all fairness, impoverished couples don't always choose to over-procreate but lack birth control options. Thus society must share the blame for over-procreation when denying couples access to modern birth control.

We hear from those who oppose abortions-on-demand, but it's time we here from those who oppose babies-on-demand. It's time to look beyond the smoke screens of religious conditioning and take a look at what's happening here on earth. A prerequisite of moral behavior is to take personal responsibility for an eco-friendly planet. To harm the planet is to vandalize the home of all living things we know; and overpopulation is certainly doing just that. So if a religion says that it is all right for the world population to continue growing, then that religion is wrong.

So when is it moral to have children? This is a question society doesn't ask, but should. Society talks about overpopulation generically, as if overpopulation is caused by "they." Perhaps many of the world's problems would be solved if we were to address these in the first and second person: you, me, we, us, instead of that generic, undefined "they." An analogy here is traffic jams. Every person on the road contributes to that jam but blames the traffic on everyone else. And most everyone stuck in that jam is waiting for their government to take care of the problem rather than accepting any personal responsibility for reducing the traffic.

Likewise, many people are waiting for a deity or savior to come here and fix all of our man-made problems rather than people working together to fix the problems that mankind has caused. Why would any deity want to help such a stupid lot of people who won't solve their own self-made problems? It is certainly not a sign of mature behavior to wait around for someone to solve the problems that we ourselves can solve. And overpopulation should be one of the easiest problems to solve because we know what causes the problem and we know how to fix it. So why aren't we fixing it?

One reason is the gender bias of religions. Religions are *man*-made, and thus prone to sexism and the oppression of women, especially with their outdated philosophy: Be fruitful and multiply. Followers of these religions argue that it's wrong to not have children. It's time to ask if it is wrong to *have* children. Or to paraphrase, is it wrong for people to have however many children they want? Another reason we're not fixing the problem is that there is still the overwhelming urge to reproduce one's genes, and also because the drive for genetic reproduction is sometimes stronger than the desire to raise children. Apparently, staying home and raising children seems too dull an occupation for many women; and men don't seem eager to take on this job.

And yet another reason our species has failed to prevent population growth is that not everyone is able to connect the dots between what they read, hear and see in the media, and population size. It is unfortunate that there are still people who don't think global warming is real. The people who have already lost their homes to global warming know just how real it is.

Global warming claims first inhabited island [1]

"For the first time, an inhabited island has disappeared beneath rising seas. Environment Editor Geoffrey Lean reports" Published: 24 December 2006 Independent (London)

"Rising seas, caused by global warming, have for the first time washed an inhabited island off the face of the Earth. The obliteration of Lohachara island, in India's part of the Sundarbans where the Ganges and the Brahmaputra rivers empty into the Bay of Bengal, marks the moment when one of the most apocalyptic predictions of environmentalists and climate scientists has started coming true.

"As the seas continue to swell, they will swallow whole island nations, from the Maldives to the Marshall Islands, inundate vast areas of countries from Bangladesh to Egypt, and submerge parts of scores of coastal cities.

"Eight years ago, as exclusively reported in The Independent on Sunday, the first uninhabited islands — in the Pacific atoll nation of Kiribati — vanished beneath the waves. The people of low-lying islands in Vanuatu, also in the Pacific, have been evacuated as a precaution, but the land still juts above the sea. The disappearance of Lohachara, once home to 10,000 people, is unprecedented."

And for those Americans whose arrogance leads them to believe that the United States is invincible, Fox News (online) carries this item from the Associated Press, June 1, 2006: *Part of New Orleans Sinking More than Once Thought:*

---

1 CLIMACTION Wednesday, December 27, 2006. *Global warming claims first inhabited island* http://climaction.blogspot.com/2006/12/global-warming-claims-first-inhabited.html

"WASHINGTON — Everyone has known New Orleans is a sinking city. Now new research suggests parts of the city are sinking even faster than many scientists imagined — more than an inch a year.

"That may explain some of the levee failures during Hurricane Katrina and it raises more worries about the future.

"The research, reported in the journal *Nature*, is based on new satellite radar data for the three years before Katrina struck in 2005. The data show that some areas are sinking four or five times faster than the rest of the city. And that, experts say, can be deadly.

"'My concern is the very low-lying areas,' said lead author Tim Dixon, a University of Miami geophysicist. "I think those areas are death traps. I don't think those areas should be rebuilt.'"[1]

And from the *Philadelphia Inquirer*, Aug 31, 2012

"[T]he Louisiana coast is steadily eroding due to rising sea levels, oil drilling and even levee building that stops spring floods from replenishing marshes. The state has lost about 1,900 square miles of land since the 1930s, and scientists warn that more will follow."[2]

The causes of this phenomenon called subsidence (the gradual sinking of landforms to a lower level), include over-development. Overpopulation results in overdeveloped cities and loss of pristine land. Remember, the human population of Earth roughly quadrupled in size during the twentieth century and is still growing; however, our planet remains virtually the same size. And according to Ocean Planet Smithsonian, "The oceans cover 71 percent of the Earth's surface and contain 97 percent of the Earth's water. Less

---

1 Fox News.com, Jun 6, 2001, Associated Press, *Part of New Orleans Sinking More than Once Thought* http://www.foxnews.com/story/0,2933,197665,00.html
2 *Philadelphia Inquirer*, Aug 31, 2012, *Isaac renews old debate about Louisiana levees* by Cain Burdeau, Associated Press http://www.philly.com/philly/wires/ap/news/nation/20120831_ap_isaacrenewsolddebateaboutlouisianalevees.html

than 1 percent is fresh water, and 2-3 percent is contained in glaciers and ice caps."[1]

Furthermore, much of Earth's land is uninhabitable, such as rugged mountains, scorched deserts, and temperatures not suited to human civilization.

Earth has so many serious problems, many of which could be solved or at least somewhat mitigated through a reduction in the birth rate. Here are some of the problems aggravated by the population growth of this past century. These problems overlap or feed upon one another, but they are all symptomatic of an overpopulated world:

- Air pollution
- Animal cruelty
- Decreased nutrition in food
- Endangered species
- Energy shortages
- Environmental destruction
- Fewer trees and fewer pristine places
- Food shortages
- Increased government regulation
- Increased pesticides in food
- Increased violence and other crime
- Inflation
- Long daily commutes to work
- Loss of privacy
- Mass-produced products resulting in decreased quality
- More job competition
- New taxes
- Over-crowded jails
- Over-developed cities
- Respiratory problems
- Stress

---

1 "OCEAN PLANET" OCEANOGRAPHIC FACTS, Judith Gradwohl, Smithsonian Institution (Curator/Ocean Planet) http://seawifs.gsfc.nasa.gov/OCEAN_PLANET/HTML/education_oceanographic_facts.html

- Suburban sprawl
- Traffic

Reducing the human birth rate is the pragmatic approach to solving overpopulation.

Pragmatism:

1. a practical approach to problems and affairs

2. an American movement in philosophy founded by C.S. Pierce and William James and marked by the doctrine that the meaning of conceptions is to be sought in their practical bearings, that the function of thought is to guide action, and that truth is preeminently to be tested by the practical consequences of belief.[1]

So to summarize: morally correct behavior is (1) based on the here and now; (2) provides the greatest good and reduces world suffering; (3) and seeks truth through the practical consequences of belief. With this is mind, the suffering being inflicted globally by over-procreation, and by the impractical consequences of this suffering, leads the intelligent mind to recognize unrestrained procreation as an immoral act.

Over-procreators violate the rights of everyone else to breathe clean air; to have sufficient food and energy resources at prices we can all afford; and to reside in livable cities with nice neighborhoods. Today's cities are subject to over-development and suburban sprawl, both of which are undermining their livability. Over-procreation seriously undermines our planet's sustainability and our own sustainability. Those who over procreate are a threat to the rights and safety of the rest of us. Having a child is not a personal matter. It is a global matter. We have the right to defend our world and ourselves from the harm inflicted upon us by those who over procreate.

Unfortunately, some adults appear unable to comprehend world problems. If they are not mature enough to care about the world in which we all live, then they are not mature enough to be

---

1   Merriam-Webster   Online   http://www.merriam-webster.com/dictionary/pragmatism

bringing up children. And it is a misconception that parents are the best judge of what is right for their children. Many children have parents in jail or on drugs or just too busy to do good parenting. Many children have parents who regret being parents. And parents are not generally objective regarding their own children.

Parents bring children into the world with an image of what they want their children to be and all too often that image is a mirror-image of themselves. Parents often try to relive their own lives and dreams through their children. In a way, they view their children as the reincarnation of themselves. This said, we are born free into a world that confines us right from the start.

So when is it moral to have children? It is easier to determine when it is *not* moral to have children because moral behavior is based on what we know, not what we *don't* know. We do know that it is immoral to contribute to a birth rate that contributes to an increase in the world population. And know this! Parents do not have a moral right to determine the religion, politics, careers or other legal lifestyle choices of their children; however, if parents can't do this they might not want children.

CHAPTER 8. A RIGHT NOT TO BE BORN

This chapter examines from a different perspective the question raised in the previous one: When is it moral to have children? Chapter 7 asks this question from an environmental and sociological perspective: what works best for life on this planet; but what about the rights of future generations, the unborn, the not yet conceived? Do future generations have a right to not be here?

The question of whether to have children is generally asked from a religious perspective or that of a couple wishing to procreate, but who speaks for the future generations? This question cannot be put to future offspring because future offspring don't yet exist, not in this world anyway; but we need to examine all the ramifications of creating a life, not just the religious dogma and egoistic side of procreation. We do know the following: to be born is to die, for death always follows birth. As sure as we are born, we die; but do we have a moral right to put others through this cycle?

Religious leaders seldom remind their parishioners that you cannot create life without also predestining death. We all know this to be true. It is a universal truth, but an unspoken one. It is "The emperor wears no clothes" type of truth.

If you never existed, then you would not be here to say if you wish to exist. You must first exist in order to evaluate that question, in order to even consider the question. Plain and simple, that which does not exist cannot regret non-existence; however, it is certainly possible for people who *do* exist to regret their existence. Many people have regretted that they were ever born.

As mentioned in Chapter 3: if you never existed, then you obviously would not have the consciousness to care whether you exist. So Descartes' axiom, "I think; therefore I am." becomes, "If I am not, then I don't think." Of course, this is not quite the same thing as saying, "I don't think; therefore I am not."

When parents divorce, the courts are supposed to determine child custody based on what is best for the children. Yet there are few laws in place to consider whether a couple should have children in the first place. Is this not analogous to doling out punishment for a crime that has been committed while doing nothing to prevent that crime in the first place? This is not to say that having a baby is by definition a crime; but it is a crime for people to have children when they are not prepared to do a good job of parenting. We don't blame dumb animals for procreating because they are acting from instinct rather than intelligence; but humans should act from intelligence rather than instinct in their decision whether to procreate. If humans don't use their intelligence, then what's the point of having it?

Now let's consider the "expressivist objection" on eugenics put forth by some advocates for the disabled. This argument is that it is generally wrong for women to "screen out" defective fetuses because this is a form of eugenics and sends the message that disabled people should not exist.[1]Advocacy

---

1 Oxford Scholarship Online, Stephen Wilkinson, Contributor http://www.oxfordscholarship.com/view/10.1093/acprof:oso/9780199273966.001.0001/acprof-9780199273966-chapter-6 "The Eugenics Argument says that screening out disability is wrong because it is a form of eugenics. This chapter defends the view that this argument cannot overcome certain problems: notably the fact that, on the most sensible definitions of 'eugenics', eugenics is not necessarily wrong. However, it should be noted that there are objectionable forms of eugenics (e.g.,those which attempt to pass off racism or 'genetic discrimination' as 'genetic improvement'). The Expressivist Argument says that what is wrong with selecting out disability is that it sends out a negative and damaging message: that the world would be a better place if people with disabilities did not exist. It

groups for the disabled see themselves as a minority group requiring protection against discrimination. Disabled persons argue, and correctly so, that there is more to them than just their disabilities and that they don't want to be identified by their disabilities. They are not necessarily opposed to abortion on principle; however, they oppose abortion for the above reason. They might approve abortion if it will prevent a lifetime of suffering.

This expressivist objection is valid in so far as people with disabilities don't wish to be targeted for discrimination, but what it does not tell us is the level of suffering that disabled individuals might find intolerable. We all have our breaking points. The expressivist objection to prenatal screening could also be deemed less than altruistic if it is about bringing disabled people into the world in order to bolster the size of the disabled population for political clout. The *Americans With Disabilities Act*, handicapped parking spaces and wheelchair accessible buildings are some of the important work that organizations for the disabled have accomplished; but these organizations are not justified in opposing the prevention of birth defects via prenatal screening and abortion.

This would constitute sex discrimination akin to that of the Religious Right, regarding a woman's body as belonging to someone other than herself. And it is difficult to argue against one form of discrimination while advocating another. To eliminate or reduce birth defects can reduce human suffering. Do organizations for people with disabilities not want to reduce human suffering? If medical intervention could cure or eliminate physical disabilities (before or after birth), would this not also be a form of eugenics? How would proponents of the expressivist argument on eugenics view this? To be consistent, they would need to oppose medical intervention here, too.

It has also been argued that eugenics is not necessarily wrong in itself if it is done to prevent suffering and not with the intention of discriminating against any group based on race or ethnicity. But

is argued that screening out does not necessarily send out a morally problematic message provided that it is done for defensible reasons (such as the avoidance of suffering) and is not presented or carried out in an insensitive way."

this raises some interesting questions: (1) How do we know in advance how much an individual might suffer, (2) What level of suffering is acceptable, and (3) Who gets to decide? These questions are to be asked here not from the wishes of the parents and, just for the moment, not even what is best for society, but rather what is in the best interest of the future individual, if born, and his or her autonomy.

How do we know in advance how much an individual might suffer? We can really only evaluate this question in terms of such qualities as the potential health of a future person (freedom from physical pain or physical restrictions) and the family circumstances into which a person will be born (opportunities during the formative years) and the political climate which prevails at the time (potential for personal autonomy at a societal level) and whether that person will have an open future (the freedom to choose his or her own future without restrictions due to adversities regarding any of the above).

What level of suffering is acceptable? If it is easier to argue against bringing disabled persons into the world than to argue against procreation for other reasons, does the former help us find answers to the latter? If we can argue that it is unfair to bring people into this world to suffer disabilities that could have been avoided through pregnancy termination, can we then also argue that it is unfair to bring people into this world who will suffer a limited future in other ways?

In order to prevent all future suffering in the world, we would need to eliminate all sentient beings (human and otherwise) from the planet, a solution not acceptable to everyone. Not all current residents of this planet would object to experiencing some suffering if given the option between that and death. And no doubt this would also have held true for members of past generations. From this we may infer that some members of future generations would also choose a degree of suffering over death. Of course, future generations must first exist before they can make this or any other decision. But how much suffering might be acceptable to them?

One person's tolerable level of suffering may be intolerable to another; leading us to conclude that this is a subjective matter unless we can find some objective clues upon which we can determine what is an acceptable level of suffering. We know that some people find life intolerable to the point of suicide or Physician Assisted Suicide (PAS). We might argue that suicides are rash decisions that could be avoided if these individuals could see their way through the problems which prompt such action. But this would not include PAS where there are many safeguards in place, such as waiting periods and counseling and where the patient must first be diagnosed as terminally ill.

Washington and Oregon states have legalized PAS for terminally ill people suffering unbearable physical pain, and for terminally ill people who want death with dignity — i.e., some control over their end-of-life situations. These are individuals who fear loss of autonomy and who don't see themselves as having any prospects for a pain-free end of life. They don't see themselves as having a future worth living. This might apply to people who have terminal cancer or who have been diagnosed with Alzheimer's.

We can also evaluate what non-terminal persons with severe disabilities consider intolerable suffering: people who make clear that they would rather not have been born in the first place. These evaluations could provide the social sciences with some objective data from which to draw conclusions about the types of pain and suffering that would render life unbearable for the majority of people; however, it would still not remove the subjective element in deciding what makes a particular individual's life unbearable. Since we cannot draw hard lines between types of suffering, then it seems that if we can screen out fetuses for one type of suffering, we should also take other forms of suffering into consideration. So this brings us to the question: Who gets to decide?

Who gets to decide whether someone should be born? Since we cannot put this question to the unborn, then we must weigh the reasons aforementioned as to how much the future individual is likely to suffer and how intolerable this future person may find life: issues of pain, physical disabilities, inheritable disease, political climate, future openness, family circumstances (e.g., parents are drug addicts, incarcerated, or living in abject poverty).

Prenatal screening can help answer questions pertaining to physical suffering; and family and societal circumstances can be evaluated as to a child's likely future autonomy; but after all this is weighed, potential parents need to realize that they might be bringing someone into the world who does not want to be here. And should parents be the only ones with the right to decide to bring new people into this world?

Procreation is circumstantial; we are all born into certain circumstances. Should the government have some say in determining the circumstances? Is this not analogous to arguing that if we choose to smoke then we must accept that this is circumstantial? For instance, the government has a duty to impose circumstances such as age requirements and to provide non-smoking areas to protect the rights and health of the rest of us. Likewise, should not the government also have a duty to prevent procreation under some circumstances: e.g., the birth of an individual overburdened with suffering, or just too many individuals causing the rest of us to suffer?

Religious leaders often want to be the ones to decide matters pertaining to procreation. Certain religions keep preaching that we don't have a right to deny birth. This keeps society from asking the opposite question: Do we really have a right to bear children? Do we really have the right to bring people into this world? It should not be at all difficult to understand why religions preach this pro-life dogma. They want to increase the size of their flocks for political clout.

In order to accomplish this, these religious leaders keep media attention focused on the 'rights' of the unborn, much as a magician focuses an audience's attention in the wrong place. This is referred to as *misdirection*. Religious leaders are magicians who misdirect the attention of their flock, especially the unsophisticated minds that are easily swayed. Religious leaders do far more preaching for the unborn than for the welfare of the born that are in need of food, clothing, shelter, education, healthcare and money. Nor do religious leaders offer a guarantee of these necessities to pregnant women who would agree to forgo abortion in exchange for such a guarantee. This anti-abortion stance, in addition to being used to bolster church membership, is also about "putting women in their place."

And nations at war want sons to fight their wars, explaining why many civilizations have favored sons over daughters. These power-hungry motives explain the "pro-life' motives of religions and governments; but children should not be born to boost the enrollment of religions or to provide cannon fodder for wars.

Chapter 7 asks the procreation question from a global perspective, but just as soon as we are born we become members of the global community and begin to form judgments about life based upon our place in this community.

So when is it morally right for children to be born? Mankind can invent religions, but this does not bring us any closer to the answer. We come into this world without knowledge of what precedes or follows our duration here. What proof do we have that life is better here than somewhere else or better than no life at all? Truth is we just don't have all the answers. So is it ever moral to have children?

We do not have a verifiable answer to this question. So should we base the answer on religious beliefs? Certainly not! Beliefs can be true or false. In the absence of indisputable knowledge concerning procreation, all we can know is that we don't bring people into existence for their own sake since people don't exist until they exist. We create people for our own interests and possibly for the interests of society, depending on society's needs.

We need to ask the question of procreation for the sake of the planet's inhabitants collectively, as well as individually. This requires governments to consider the qualifications of would-be parents' ability to raise healthy, well-cared-for children. Parents should be expected to meet an acceptable level of competence in raising their progeny. But if we set certain mental, moral and financial standards, who gets to decide these standards? What is the litmus test?

We must keep asking these questions in hopes of raising our consciousness; and because it would appear that we alone are the only species with the consciousness to ask. It has been argued by some that even a bad life is better than no life at all; but this is not an argument, merely an opinion. Those who put forth this opinion need to show us the premises that led to their conclusion. The burden of proof is on them.

And a critically important point here: adoption is not birth control. Not only does adoption fail to prevent birth, advocates of adoption fail to recognize the right of each individual to know his or her biological parents and other genetic heritage. If would-be parents prefer biological children over adopted children, doesn't it stand to reason that this works both ways: that children prefer biological parents over adopted parents? Are pro-adoption 'right-to-lifers' trying to deny children their biological parents?

It is not uncommon for children, upon learning of their adoption, to spend the rest of their lives trying to discover their biological families. Adopted children often suffer from an identity crisis. Many people like to pursue their genealogy: tracing their ancestry; however, adopted children often struggle just to learn the identity of their parents, and any siblings.

It is often the case that parents of adopted children turned to adoption when they were unable to conceive children of their own. They chose to adopt in the absence of biological children. But what choices did the children have?

Prior to 'the pill' and legal abortion, there were orphanages full of unwanted children. Where were these 'right-to-lifers' back then? How come they waited until abortion was legalized before coming out so strongly in favor of adoption? And why aren't they opening their pocketbooks to poor women/couples who have children instead of abortions? These 'right-to-lifers' should put their money where their mouths are instead of trying to cause so much misery in the world.

And let's take a look at this misnomer, 'right-to-lifers.' Are they really pro-life? Where do they stand on war, capital punishment, animal rights? Where do they stand on taxation for social programs for underprivileged children? Is *pro-life* a bit of George Orwell *newspeak*? Next time these 'right-to-lifers' pretend (or seriously believe) that they are pro-life, call them on it. Don't let them get away with their hypocrisy. Unwanted childbirth has ruined many a life. And continued population growth may be the end of all of us.

We don't know if we had a right not to be born. But if we cannot establish that the unborn have a right not to be here, likewise, we cannot establish the opposite either: We cannot establish that the unborn *do* have a right to be here. It cuts both ways.

CHAPTER 9. WORLD KARMA

We humans are up too close to the present moment (whatever that present moment may be) to be able to see the larger picture: karma. Karma is simply cause and effect, as ye sow ye shall reap, what goes around comes around. If we step back a ways and look at the larger picture, we can begin to view interesting patterns.

For instance, until relatively recent history, families were large with women bearing half a dozen or more children and there was a high infant mortality rate. It was not at all uncommon for couples to lose a few children; and women frequently died in childbirth. Women had nearly no rights, and thus had few options in life other than marriage and motherhood. Birth control was not even an acceptable topic of conversation; and the babies just kept coming.

Then with the advancement of women's rights (in parts of the world, anyway) birth control options became available, and couples started having fewer children. And perhaps as a karmic reward for this, child mortality rates decreased: the U.S. saw a 93% decrease in the 20th century between 1915 and 1998.[1] And as child mortality rates decreased, life expectancy increased; however, the birth rate is

---

1 *Child Health USA 2000:* An illustrated collection of current and historical data, published annually, "The infant mortality declined substantially during the 20th century resulting in a 93 percent decrease in the overall infant mortality rate

still far too high to achieve world equilibrium. Now, many couples are choosing to be child-free. Is this personal choice alone, or is it also global karma?

On a personal level we make choices; but nature also appears to make choices on a larger scale. Nature may be nudging us into achieving balance and harmony with the planet. It is likely that not all our choices come at the conscious level, but this does not necessarily diminish our personal freedom. What may seem like fate may simply be choices our minds have made that our consciousness does not currently perceive because we are caught up in the present moment in time. How often have people remarked that hindsight is better than foresight?

And how often have we heard that those who forget their past mistakes are doomed to repeat them? This is why historians play such a vital role in civilization. If they are honest in their work, then they try to help us see the larger picture that spans more than a personal lifetime.

There are still some half a million babies being born every day worldwide, but more and more couples are choosing not to have children.[1] They consciously choose to be child-free for any one of many reasons; but are they also tuned in to a higher consciousness that requires a drastic reduction in the birthrate if we are to save our planet? Is nature trying to save the human species from itself?

As discussed in Chapter 4, intelligent people average fewer children than not-so-intelligent people; and many geniuses have no children at all. Genius is believed to come from a higher level of consciousness; and perhaps this is why so many of history's geniuses have been child-free. Another way of stating it: geniuses have often been described as being ahead of their time. Isn't this to say that geniuses have better foresight about where human behavior is leading us?

Here is another interesting karmic pattern: until recent history, women and young girls who had babies out of wedlock faced

---

between 1915 and 1998." http://Marb. hrsa.gov/chusall/hstat/hsi/pages/205im.html

1 http://wiki.answers.com/Q/How_many_babies_are_born_every_day_in_the_world

a lifetime of ruin. Today, there are single women who are having 'sperm-bank' babies and there are young girls flaunting their out-of-wedlock babies as if making up for past generations of society's cruelty to out-of-wedlock mothers; however, two wrongs don't make a right. And children do have a right to know their biological families: maternal *and* paternal. But, this present day behavior may be a reaction to all the years that out-of-wedlock babies were the ruin of a woman.

Isaac Newton postulated, "To every action there is an equal and opposite reaction." Isn't this another expression of karma? How many ways need it be said before people catch on? We see this not only in the flaunting behavior of young girls with babies; we also see it in the feminist movement. But considering the centuries of suppression of women, how are we to interpret this equal and opposite reaction?

Could this equal and opposite reaction also be a chain reaction that is beginning to show in our environmental abuse of our planet? Isn't it high time people turn away from the dangerous politics of religion before it's too late? Yet there are organized religions that prey upon people whose minds are not strong enough to reason things out for themselves. And religious leaders who continue to preach the old adage "be fruitful and multiply" are wreaking havoc with our planet. Their power-hungry egos may be the demise of all of us if their followers continue to listen to them.

The equal-and-opposite-reaction principle is showing up in weather patterns, increased air pollution and subsequent respiratory problems and so much more. Nature itself is fighting back against too much motherhood — and too much fatherhood. Regardless of whether nature has inherent intelligence, the principles of physics still apply. It would be far better for the planet and its inhabitants if people would procreate less. Let's not test the equal-and-opposite-reaction principle where the environment is concerned. Let's not push our luck.

Speaking of chain reactions, when people have children, they set in motion a chain of events over which they have little control. People with children have some responsibility for all their descendants because without first having children it is impossible to have grandchildren, great grandchildren, etc. Yet having set in motion this chain of events, how many parents stop to consider their number of offspring that will occupy this planet even four or five generations down line, beyond their own life-expectancy and that of their children, grandchildren and perhaps great grandchildren? How many of us, with or without children, give much thought to future generations, or to past generations for that matter? Isn't hindsight supposed to improve foresight?

You might wish to argue that you are only 50% responsible for the existence of children you sire/bear (It takes two to tango) and only 25% responsible for the existence of your grandchildren; with your responsibility diminishing with each successive generation of descendants; but you don't get off the hook that easily. You have two parents, four grandparents, eight great grandparents and so forth; and, if any one of those links had been missing, you'd be missing; you would not be here. When it comes to ancestors, there are no missing links. The same is true going in the opposite direction. So you share the responsible for the existence of all your descendants.

The human population of earth roughly quadrupled in the twentieth century. And today there are over a billion more people on this planet than at the start of the twenty-first century. That's over a billion more births than the number of deaths during this same period. A more intelligent species would surely wonder why we do this to ourselves. Intelligent members of our own species are wondering the same thing. If there are people whose hindsight is so limited that they cannot reflect on this, then it is likely that their foresight is also limited. Are people so stuck in the present moment that they can't see the harm population growth is doing to our planet? For those who don't care about the planet, remember, this is not *your* planet, it is *our* planet. Earth is not yours to destroy.

And do you oppose government regulations? Regulations are a karmic outcome of population growth. They swell in tandem to population growth. If you dislike too much government interference in your life, keep in mind that as the population increases so do government regulations. Traffic lights are an obvious example of this. A large city has far more traffic lights than a small town.

Want another example? If you go out into the woods and cut down a tree, you can face fines and jail time. Population growth necessitates these kinds of restrictions on people. Not all that many years ago it was common practice for people to go out into the woods to cut a tree for the Christmas holiday. But that was when the population was much smaller. If everyone today were to cut a holiday tree, the damage to our forests would be immense.

Christmas trees aside, for each baby born, many trees are harvested for housing, furniture and paper. Further aggravating this loss of trees is the deforestation being carried out in order to clear land for raising crops and livestock, not to mention raising more humans. Individuals may not cut trees on public lands, but logging companies are allowed to do so. Our government has a double standard: one for big business and one for everyone else, and this double standard is exacerbated by population growth.

As the population grows, so does the wealth of giant corporations. And this wealth is giving big business more control over our government, and thus over us. Big business now overrides government authority on commerce (the World Trade Organization). Governments can no longer make decisions in the best interest of their people or the environment. Who empowers these giant corporations? We do. As the population increases, so does the demand for jobs and for goods. This is another karmic outcome: we give big business more consumers and more cheap labor and we pay the price.

The more of us there are, the more restrictions and regulations we face — and need; but these regulations should come from a government run by the people, not run by big business. Government regulation is not the only thing that increases with population growth. Poverty also increases. High birth rates go hand in hand with low standards of living. We see this in third world countries. "Typically, high birth rates have been associated with health impairments and low life expectancy, low living standards, low status of women, and low levels of education.[1] Our aim is not to become a third world nation, but we are getting there anyway; and population growth has much to do with it.

Metropolitan areas are becoming America's third world countries. Big cities have become home to the homeless, if you'll pardon the oxymoron. There was a time when people could claim a parcel of land and live off it. One did not need to climb the corporate ladder in order to earn a living. Many folks are not suited for the corporate world, the urban jungle; but individuals born into crowded cities often find few avenues of escape from the urban jungle. Or people migrate to the big cities seeking corporate jobs that prove to be nonexistent and end up on the streets. Job growth does not keep pace with population growth, especially when corporations strive to downsize their workforce.

"Go west, young man." And many did just that. In the mid-19th century Americans could move out west, stake out a donation land claim from the federal government and live off the land. That was then; this is now. The difference is population size. Let's look at population growth in the U.S.[2]

People living in the U.S.:

1850	23,191,876
1900	76,212,168
2000	281,421,906
2010	308,745,538

The interior U.S. is not as densely populated as the coastal areas, but that's because much of the nation's population chooses to live along coastlines. Also, much of the interior of our nation is in the hands of big business, e.g.,big corporate farms. Our government gives big corporations nearly unrestricted access to large tracts of wilderness and even builds roads and other amenities for these cor-

---

1 Wikipedia http://en.wikipedia.org/wiki/Birth_rate "Political issues."
2 U.S. Department of Commerce, Bureau of the Census http://en.wikipedia.org/wiki/United_States_Census

porations; but what is our government doing for *We the People?* Are there just too many of us for the government to tend to our needs?

With an escalating world population, the quality of life is declining; but is the quality of people also declining? Is quality being exchanged for quantity? What happened to the days when people did not have to lock their doors? Nowadays, the papers are full of reports on violent crimes on college campuses, in public schools, at shopping malls, and on the streets even in broad daylight. Counties keep building more jails as the population increases and as parental guidance decreases.

Many parents don't seem to know or care where their children are, and many young people hang out on the streets. Why aren't they at home doing schoolwork, housework or other chores? If parents want children, why then aren't they raising them? Undisciplined children are being dumped on society. Perhaps too many women want motherhood plus a career outside the home. Then when they find that this doesn't work as they thought it would, the children get pushed into the background.

The world today is full of troubled children and children in trouble. It seems both parents want exciting careers and neither one wants to stay home and "mind the kids." The two-career family may have more money to spend on their children than the one-career family but less time. Has money become a substitute for parenting? Children are being spoiled with mass-produced toys, clothes, computers, phones, etc. Is this to camouflage parents' guilt for not spending more time with their children?

But there is that stubborn question that is not going away: Why are people having children if they can't be bothered raising them or just don't have the time?

Prior to today's gluttony of gadgets, there was family time. The family would climb into their one vehicle and go for a Sunday drive out into the countryside, perhaps stopping to buy fresh produce at a small farm just outside the city. Mothers could send their children outdoors to play with neighbor children, where nearby vacant lots offered creative opportunities not to be found in formal parks full of expensive playground equipment. Everything today is so overprogrammed. Today's urban child may not experience the Sunday drive in the countryside, the nearby small farms with their fresh produce, nor the vacant lots where children's imaginations could provide hours of free fun and entertainment.

Households now have multiple vehicles, where just one used to suffice; the countryside is now an extension of the city: more houses and buildings; and the small farms on the outskirts of town have been replaced with suburbs. Today's food in grown on agri-farms: vast stretches of land heavily inundated with pesticides, and crops that are picked green so as to be shipped hundreds of miles, and then dyed or waxed to make them look more appealing.

Cities today have few vacant lots where children's imaginations and feet can run free, where they can pick wild flowers or wild berries. And all the traffic makes it unsafe for children to walk to school these days: yesterday's residential streets are today's arterials. Nor do children play hide 'n seek and other fresh air games. They have their TVs and computers sans fresh air; but then the air is no longer all that fresh anyway.

Many parents, wishing to escape the overbuilt inner cities, move their families to the suburbs. But they can't escape their problems there because they themselves are the problem. All of us are the problem because there are just too many of us. A return to yesteryear's quality of life would require a return to yesteryear's population size. And even then, it would take many years to reclaim our planet, to regrow our forests, to clean the air and water, and to relearn civility.

Overpopulation is bad karma on a global scale. It would not be so bad if it only affected those who are responsible for the problem. Unfortunately, even small families and the child-free suffer the consequences of an overpopulated planet. If the burden were to fall only on those who are to blame, then the guilty parties would more likely see the harm they are causing.

We need a moratorium on births. We need to restructure our tax system. The individual who has more than two children during his/her lifetime should pay a tax that would benefit individuals who are child-free, or who have only one child. Individuals with two children would neither pay nor benefit from this tax. They would be considered environmentally neutral, provided they remain child-free at least until their thirties. This tax would be imposed on parents for the duration of their lives, unless their children predecease them.

- Remember, if you have a child it is not just your business. It is everyone's business. Your child is part of the world in which we all live. To quote the nineteenth century conservationist, John Muir (honored on the California state 25-cent coin): "When one tugs at a single thing in nature, he finds it attached to the rest of the world."[1]

- Since overpopulation is a severe and life threatening problem, to contribute to overpopulation is immoral. It is immoral to aggravate the environmental problems of the planet that is home to all life we know. There are two means by which the human population increases: (1) high birth rate and (2) extended life-span. To limit the life-span would require killing people off by a certain age. The other means of population control is preferable: curtail the birth rate.

- When you see a large family, take a moment to consider that this is why we pay higher utility bills, higher grocery bills, higher rent or mortgage. And there is only one intelligent, moral way to reduce the size of the *Homo sapiens* population: birth control.

Table 1: Famous Women Who Didn't Have Children

Emma Abbott: Opera soprano
b. Dec 9, 1850 Chicago IL
d. Jan 5, 1891 Salt Lake City UT

Jane Addams: Social reformer; Nobel Peace Prize winner
    1931
b. 1860 Cedarville IL
d. 1935 Chicago IL

Maria Gaetana Agnesi: Mathematician; author of *Analytical
    Institutions*
b. May 16, 1718 Milan, Italy
d. Jan 9, 1799 Milan, Italy

Maria Teresa Agnesi (a.k.a. d'Agnesi): Composer, librettist,
    harpsichordist, singer
b. Oct 17, 1720 Milan, Italy
d. Jan 19, 1795 Milan, Italy

Zoe Akins: Playwright, screenwriter, 1935 Pulitzer Prize
b. Oct 30, 1886 Humansville MO
d. Oct 29, 1958 Los Angeles CA

Louisa May Alcott: Author, *Little Women*
b. Nov 29, 1832 Germantown PA
d. Mar 6, 1888 Boston MA

Frances Alda: Opera soprano, NY *Metropolitan Opera*
b. May 31, 1879 Christchurch, New Zealand
d. Sep 18, 1952 Venice, Italy

Marian Anderson: Opera singer: contralto
b. Feb 27, 1897 Philadelphia PA
d. Apr 8, 1993 Portland OR

Susan B. Anthony: Abolitionist; suffragist
b. Feb 15, 1820 Adams MA
d. Mar 13, 1906 Rochester NY

Hannah Arendt: Political theorist
b. Oct 14, 1906 Hanover, Germany
d. Dec 4, 1975 New York City NY

Diana Athill: Literary editor, novelist and memoirist, *Somewhere Towards the End*
b. Dec 21, 1917 Norfolk, England

Winifred Atwell: International pianist of boogie woogie and ragtime music
b. Feb 27, 1914 Tunapuna, Trinidad
d. Feb 28, 1983 Seaforth, Sydney, Australia

Jane Austen: English Novelist, *Pride and Prejudice*
b. Dec 16, 1775 Steventon, Hampshire, England
d. Jul 18, 1817 Winchester, England

Mildred Bailey: American jazz singer, honored on US postage stamp
b. Jan 1, 1907 Tekoa WA
d. Dec 12, 1951 Poughkeepsie NY

Emily Greene Balch: Nobel Peace Prize, 1946, US; *Women's Int'l League for Peace and Freedom*
b. Jan 8, 1867 Boston MA
d. Jan 9, 1961 Cambridge MA

Amy Ballinger: Centenarian, union organizer, comedienne, Pittsburgh councilwoman
b. Apr 2, 1909 PA
d. Apr 1, 2010 Palm Beach FL

Rose Bampton: Opera soprano, NY *Metropolitan Opera* and other opera houses
b. Nov 28, 1907 Lakewood OH
d. Aug 21, 2007 Bryn Mawr PA

Tallulah Bankhead: Movie actress
b. Jan 31, 1902 Huntsville AL
d. Dec 12, 1968 New York NY

Theda Bara: Silent screen actress honored on US postage stamp
b. Jul 29, 1885 Avondale OH
d. Apr 7, 1955 Los Angeles CA

Lady Evelyn (Rothwell) Barbirolli: Oboe soloist, *London Royal Symphony*
b. Jan 24, 1911 Wallingford-on-Thames, Englaand
d. Jan 25, 2008 London, England

Clarissa "Clara" Barton: Founder of *American Red Cross*; feminist
b. Dec 25, 1821 North Oxford MA
d. Apr 12, 1912 Glen Echo MD

Katherine Lee Bates: Author, poet, wrote lyrics to *America the Beautiful*
b. Aug 12, 1859 Falmouth MA
d. Mar 28, 1929 Wellesley MA

Kathy Bates: Oscar winning actress
b. Jun 28, 1948 Memphis TN

Amy Beach: Composer, pianist, first woman to perform
with *Boston Symphony*
b. Sep 5, 1867 Henniker NH
d. Dec 27, 1944 New York NY

Simone de Beauvoir: Author; philosopher
b. Jan 9, 1908 Paris, France
d. Apr 14, 1986 Paris, France

Dame Heather Begg: International opera mezzo-soprano
b. Dec 1, 1932 Nelson, New Zealand
d. May 12, 2009 Sydney, Australia

Gertrude Bell: Archeologist; writer, mideast political analyst; founded Baghdad museum
b. Jul 14, 1868 Washington Hall, County Durham, England
d. Jul 12, 1926 Baghdad, Iraq

Ruth Benedict: Anthropologist and author
b. Jun 5, 1887 Shenango Valley NY
d. Sep 17, 1948 New York NY

Charlotte Benkner: Oldest living person
b. Nov 16, 1889 Leipzig, Germany
d. May 14, 2004 North Lima OH

Svetlana Beriosova: Ballerina, *London Royal Ballet* and other
companies
b. Sep 24, 1932 Kaunas, Lithuania
d. Nov 10, 1998 Kensington, London

Ruth Bernhard: Pioneer woman photographer; lived to 101
b. 1905 Berlin, Germany
d. Dec 18, 2006 San Francisco CA

Julie Winnefred Bertrand: Named world's oldest woman
b. Sep 15/16, 1891 Coaticook, Canada
d. Jan 18, 2007 Montreal, Quebec, Canada

Natalia Bessmertnova: Ballerina, *Bolshoi Ballet*
b. Jul 19, 1941 Moscow, Russia
d. Feb 19, 2008 Moscow, Russia

MaVynee Betsch: Famous environmentalist known as *Beach Lady*
b. Jan 13, 1935 Jacksonville FL
d. Sep 5, 2005 American Beach FL

Hildegard Bingen a.k.a. St. Hildegard of Bingen: Writer, composer, philosopher, mystic, herbalist
b. Sep 16, 1098 Bockelheim, Germany
d. Sep 17, 1179 Rupertsberg, Germany

Jacqueline Bisset: Movie actress
b. Sep 13, 1944 Weybridge, England

Elizabeth Blackwell: First woman physician in the US
b. Feb 3, 1821 Bristol, England
d. May 31, 1910 Hastings, England

Emily Blackwell: Physician
b. Oct 8, 1826 Bristol, England
d. Sep 7, 1910 York Cliffs ME

Nellie Bly (a.k.a. Elizabeth Cochrane): Extraordinary journalist, adventurer
b. May 5, 1864 Cochran's Mills PA
d. Jan 27, 1922 New York, NY

Rosa Bonheur: Artist, famous painter of animals
b. Mar 16, 1822 Bordeaux, France
d. May 25, 1899 Chateau de By, France

Margaret Bourke-White: Famous photo-journalist, *Life Magazine*
b. Jun 14, 1904 Bronx NY
d. Aug 21, 1971 Darien CT

Marie Bremont: Lived over 115 years
b. Apr 25, 1886 Noellet, France
d. Jun 6, 2001 Candé, Maine-et-Loire (near Paris)

Anne Bronte: English novelist
b. Jan 17, 1820 Thornton, Yorkshire, England
d. May 28, 1849 Haworth, Yorkshire, England

Emily Bronte: English novelist
b. Jul 30, 1818 Thornton, Yorkshire, England
d. Dec 19, 1848 Haworth, Yorkshire, England

Louise Brooks: Actress, silent movies
b. Nov 14, 1906 Cherryvale KS
d. Aug 8, 1985 Rochester NY

Gertrude Foster Brown: Suffragist, mgr of *The Woman Citi-zen* journal, pianist with the *Berlin Philharmonic*
b. Jul 29, 1867 Morrison IL
d. Mar 1, 1956 Westport CT

Helen Gurley Brown: Writer; editor *Cosmopolitan Magazine*
b. Feb 18, 1922 Green Forest Arkansas
d. Aug 13, 2012 New York NY

Margaret Wise Brown; Authored over a hundred children's
books, *Goodnight Moon*
b. May 23, 1910 Brooklyn NY
d. Nov 13, 1952 Nice, France

Rosina Buckman: Opera soprano
b. Mar 16, 1881 Blenheim, New Zealand
d. Dec 31, 1948 London, England

Betty Buckley: Actress singer, Movie, *Carrie*, TV, *Eight is
Enough*, Broadway: *Cats*
b. Jul 3, 1947 Ft. Worth TX

Octavia Butler: Pioneer black female sci-fi writer
b. Jun 22, 1947 Pasadena CA
d. Feb 24, 2006 Seattle WA

Patricia Dwinnell Butler: Ground-breaking woman legal ad-visor to U.S. Presidents and at the U.S. Dept. of Justice,
founding editor of what is now the Federal Register
b. Dec 23, 1907 Brooklyn NY
d. May 27, 2009 La Jolla CA

Laura Carmichael: Hundredth birthday, living in own
house, and still active
b. Nov 20, 1905 Altoona AL
d. Jan 14, 2007 Gainesville FL
Gainesville (Florida) Sun, Jan 18, 2007

Mary Cassatt: Artist, Impressionist painter
b. May 22, 1844 Allegheny City PA
d. Jun 14, 1926 Beaufresne, France

Willa Cather: Novelist, Pulitzer Prize 1923, *One of Ours*
b. Dec 7, 1873 Back Creek Valley NE
d. Apr 24, 1947 New York NY

Carrie Chapman Catt: Founder of *League of Women Voters*
b. Jan 9, 1859 Ripon WI
d. Mar 9, 1947 New Rochelle NY

Margaret Cavendish, Duchess of Newcastle: Writer,
feminist
b. 1623 Colchester, Essex, England
d. Dec 15, 1673 Welbeck Abbey, Nottinghamshire, England

Laura Cereta: Intellectual, feminist, taught philosophy at
Univ. of Prada
b. 1469 Brescia, Italy
d. 1499 Brescia, Italy

Coco Chanel: Fashion designer; perfumes
b. Aug 19, 1883 Saumur, France
d. Jan 10, 1971 Paris, France

Stockard Channing: Actress, stage and screen
b. Feb 13, 1944 New York NY

Kalpana Chawla: Astronaut
b. Mar 17, 1962 Karnal, Haryana, India
d. Feb 1, 2003 over Texas

Mary Boykin Miller Chesnut: Civil War diary; honored on
US postage stamp
b. Mar 31, 1823 Pleasant Hill SC

d. Nov 22, 1886 Camden SC

Vivian Della Chiesa: Opera Singer and radio and television
    hostess
b. Sep 15, 1915 Chicago IL
d. Jan 6, 2009 Huntington NY

Julia Child: World renowned chef
b. Aug 15, 1912 Pasadena CA
d. Aug 13, 2004 Santa Barbara CA

Shirley Chisholm: First black woman elected to Congress
b. Nov 30, 1924 New York NY
d. Jan 1, 2005 Ormond Beach FL

Imogene Coca: Comedienne
b. Nov 18, 1908 Philadelphia PA
d. Jun 2, 2001 Westport CT

Janet Collins: First principal black ballet dancer at *Metro-
    politan Opera*; broke ballet color line
b. Mar 7, 19917 New Orleans LA
d. May 28, 2003 Fort Worth TX

Imogen Cooper: Concert pianist
b. Aug 28, 1949 London, England

Prudence Crandall: Teacher opened first school in Canter-
    bury CT for black girls
b. Sep 3, 1803 Hopkinton RI
d. Jan 28, 1890 Elk Falls KS

Regine Crespin: French opera star (soprano)
b. Feb 23, 1927 Marseilles, France
d. Jul 4, 2007 Paris, France

Celia Cruz: Cuban-American singer; multiple Grammy
    winner
b. Oct 21, 1925 Havana, Cuba
d. Jul 16, 2003 Fort Lee NJ

Jean Dalrymple: American theatrical publicist, producer, playwright, director
b. Sep 2, 1902 Morristown, NJ
d. Nov 15, 1998 New York NY

Alexandra Danilova: Ballerina
b. Nov 20, 1903 Peterhof, Russia
d. Jul 13, 1997 Manhatten, NY

Dolores Del Rio: Mexican American film actress
b. Aug 3, 1905 Durango, Mexico
d. Apr 11, 1983 Newport Beach, California,

Kate DiCamillo: Author of children's books: *Winn-Dixie, The Tiger Rising*
b. Mar 25, 1964 Philadelphia, PA

Emily Dickinson: American poet
b. 1830 Amhurst MA
d. 1886 Amhurst MA

Isak Dinesen a.k.a. Karen Blixen: Author, *Out of Africa*
b. Apr 17, 1885 Zealand Island, Denmark
d. Sep 7, 1962 Rungstedlund, Denmark

Dorothea Dix: Social reformer; advocate for the poor and mentally handicapped
b. Apr 4, 1802 Hampden ME
d. Jul 17, 1887 Trenton NJ

Dorothy Dix: Pioneer advice columnist; newspaper editor
b. Nov 18, 1861 Woodstock Plantation TN
d. Dec 16, 1951 New Orleans LA

Doris Dodman: Celebrated hundredth birthday in good health; former dancer and model
b. Feb 2, 1907 Kennington, England

Felia Doubrovska: Balanchine ballerina
b. 1896 St. Petersburg, Russia
d. Sep 18, 1981 New York NY

Anne Ophelia Todd Dowden: Botanical artist, author, illustrator
b. Sep 17, 1907 Denver CO
d. Jan 11, 2007 Boulder CO

Emma Eames: Opera soprano, *New York Met* and *London Royal Opera House*
b. Aug 13, 1865 Shanghai, China
d. Jun 13, 1952 New York City

Amelia Earhart: Aviator
b. Jul 24, 1897 Atchison KS
d. Jul 1937 over Pacific Ocean?

Gertrude Ederle: First woman to swim the English Channel; Olympic gold medal 1924
b. Oct 23, 1906 New York NY
d. Nov 30, 2003 Wyckoff, NJ

Gertrude B. Elion: Nobel Prize for physiology/medicine, 1988 US
b. Jan 23, 1918 New York NY
d. Feb 21, 1999 Chapel Hill NC

Elizabeth Ellet: Historian, *The Women of the American Revolution*, 3 volumes
b. Oct 1812/1818? Sodus Point NY
d. Jun 3, 1877 New York NY

Mary Ellis: Opera singer, stage actress; lived to be 105
b. Jun 15, 1897 New York NY
d. Jan 30, 2003 London, England

Mary Ann Evans (a.k.a. George Eliot): English novelist
b. Nov 22, 1819 Chilvers Coton, England
d. Dec 22, 1880 London, England

Dame Edith Evans: British stage actress
b. Feb 8, 1888 London, England
d. Oct 14, 1976 Cranbrook, England

Oriana Fallaci: International journalist

b. Jun 29, 1929 Florence, Italy
d. Sep 15, 2006 Florence, Italy

Geraldine Farrar: Opera soprano, NY *Metropolitan Opera*, often paired with Enrico Caruso
b. Feb 28, 1882 Melrose MA
d. Mar 11, 1967 Ridgefield CT

Suzanne Farrell: Ballerina NYC *Ballet Company*
b. Aug 16, 1945 Cincinnati OH

Edna Ferber: Novelist, playwright, Pulitzer Prize 1925
b. Aug 15, 1885 Kalamazoo MI
d. Apr 16, 1968 New York NY

Lynn Fontanne: American theatre actress over 40 years
b. Dec 6, 1887 Woodford UK
d. Jul 30, 1983 Genesee Depot WI

Celia Franca: British ballet soloist; founded *National Ballet of Canada*
b. Jun 25, 1921 London, England
d. Feb 19, 2007 Ottawa, Ontario, Canada

Gyo Fujikawa: Authored multi-racial children's literature, before it was politically correct
b. Nov 3, 1908 Berkley CA
d. Nov 26, 1998 New York NY

Amelita Galli-Curci: Opera soprano
b. Nov 18, 1882 Milan, Italy
d. Nov 26, 1963 La Jolla CA

Greta Garbo: Actress, films
b. Sep 18, 1905 Stockholm, Sweden
d. Apr 15, 1990 New York, NY

Helen Hamilton Gardener: Writer, suffragist, US Civil Service Commission (1st woman)
b. 1853 Winchester VA
d. 1925 Washington D. C.

Ava Gardner: Actress, films
b. Dec 24, 1922 Smithfield NC
d. Jan 25, 1990 London, England

Helen Gaskell: Oboist with the *BBC Symphony Orchestra*
b. Jan 14, 1906 Twickenham, England
d. Oct 7, 2002 Tring, Hertfordshire, England

Elizabeth George: Novelist
b. Feb 26, 1949 Warren OH

Zelma Watson George: Alternate delegate to U.N., opera
    singer, speaker, educator
b. Dec 8, 1903 Hearn TX
d. Jul 3, 1994 Shaker Heieghts OH

Althea Gibson: Tennis champion, first black woman to win
    at Wimbledon
b. Aug 25, 1927 Silver SC
d. Sep 28, 2003 East Orange NJ

Lillian Gish: Silent screen actress
b. Oct 14, 1893 Springfield, OH
d. Feb 27, 1993 New York, NY

Ellen Glasgow: Novelist, Pulitzer Prize 1942, *In This Our Life*
b. Apr 22, 1873 Richmond VA
d. Nov 21, 1945 Richmond VA

Mary Jayne Gold: Rescued Jewish and anti-Nazi artists
    from occupied France
b. 1909 Chicago IL
d. Oct 5, 1997 St. Tropez, France

Frances Goodrich: Playwright, Pulitzer for *Diary of Anne
    Frank*; Screenwriter, *The Thin Man*
b. Dec 21, 1890 Belleville NJ
d. Jan 29, 1984 New York City NY
(see entry for husband, Albert Hackett)

Martha Graham: Dancer-choreographer, modern ballet
b. May 11, 1894 Pittsburgh PA

d. Apr 1, 1991 New York NY

Lucile Grahn: Ballerina of the Romantic period
b. Jun 30, 1819 Copenhagen, Denmark
d. Apr 4, 1907 Munich, Germany

Kate Greenaway: British artist, illustrator, author of verse
b. Mar 17, 1846 London, England
d. Nov 6, 1901 London, England

Marion Lucy Mahony Griffin: Artist, architect; worked for
    Frank Lloyd Wright
b. Feb 14, 1871 Chicago Il
d. Aug 10, 1961 Chicago IL
(see entry for Walter Burley Griffin)

Sarah Grimke: Social reformer, feminist, abolitionist, public
    speaker
b. Nov 26, 1792 Charleston SC
d. Dec 23, 1873 Hyde Park MA

Grace Groner: Humanitarian, frugal centenarian leaves
    $7,000,000 to college
b. Apr 4, 1909 Lake Co. IL
d. Jan 19, 2010 Lake Forest IL

Alice Hamilton: Pioneer doctor in industrial medicine
b. Feb 27, 1869 New York NY
d. Sep 22, 1970 Hadlyme CT

Edith Hamilton: Greek scholar, educator, writer
b. Aug 12, 1867 Dresden, Germany
d. May 31, 1963 Washington DC

Patricia Roberts Harris: First African American Woman
    named to a presidential cabinet
b. May 31, 1924 Mattoon IL
d. Mar 23, 1985 Washington D. C.

Edith Heath: Renowned ceramicist, founder of *Heath
    Ceramics*
b. May 25, 1911 Ida Grove IA

d. Dec 27, 2005 Tiburon CA

Anne Hebert: Novelist, poet, playwright
b. Aug 1, 1916 Sainte-Catherine-de-Fossambault, Quebec
d. Jan 22, 2000 Montreal, Quebec

Lillian Hellman: Playwright, *The Little Foxes, The Children's Hour*
b. Jun 20, 1905 New Orleans LA
d. Jun 30, 1984 Martha's Vineyard MA

Sonja Henie: Olympic Gold Medal figure skater; movie actress
b. Apr 8, 1912 Oslo, Norway
d. Oct 12, 1969 en route from Paris to Oslo

Katherine Hepburn: Movie actress
b. May 12, 1907 Hartford CT
d. Jun 30, 2003 Old Saybrook CT

Billie Holiday: American blues and jazz singer
b. Apr 7, 1915? Philadelphia PA
d. Jul 17, 1959 New York NY

Eleanor Holm: Olympic swimmer, gold medalist 1932
b. Dec 6, 1913 New York NY
d. Jan 31, 2004 Miami FL

Admiral Grace Murray Hopper: Pioneer computer scientist
b. Dec 9, 1906 New York NY
d. Jan 1, 1992 Arlington VA

Souad Hosni: Egyptian film actress
b. Jan 26, 1942 Cairo, Egypt
d. Jun 21, 2001 London, England

Grace Carpenter Hudson: Portrait painter of Pomo Indian children
b. Feb 21, 1865 Ukiah, Potter Valley CA
d. Mar 23, 1937 Ukiah, Potter Valley CA

Danièle Huillet: French film maker

b. May 1, 1936 Paris, France
d. Oct 9, 2006 Cholet, France

Laura Archera Huxley: Writer, concert violinist (musical
    prodigy)
b. Nov 2, 1911 Turin, Italy
d. Dec 13, 2007 Los Angeles CA

Ramona Trinidad Iglesias-Jordan: Lived to 114
b. Aug 31, 1889 7:00 AM Utuado, Puerto Rico
d. May 29, 2004 Rio Piedras, San Juan, Puerto Rico

Molly Ivins: Political columnist
b. Aug 30, 1944 Monterey CA
d. Jan 31, 2007 Austen TX

Mahalia Jackson: Gospel singer; honored on US postage
    stamp
b. Oct 26, 1912 New Orleans LA
d. Jan 27, 1972 Chicago IL

Judith Jamison: Dancer; choreographer, director of *Alvin
    Ailey Dance Company*
b. May 10, 1943 Philadelphia PA

Anna Jarvis: Founded Mother's Day Holiday, but regretted
    its commercialism
b. May 1, 1864 Grafton WV
d. Nov 24, 1948 West Chester PA

Dr. Carole Jordan: First woman president of the, *Royal Astro-
    nomical Society*
b. Jul 19, 1941 Pinner Middlesex, England

Elena Kagan: U.S. Supreme Court Justice
b. April 28, 1960 New York City NY

Frida Kahlo: Artist, painter influenced by indigenous
    cultures
b. Jul 6, 1907 Mexico City, Mexico
d. Jul 13, 1954 Mexico City, Mexico

Yue-Sai Kan: Chinese-American TV personality, entrepreneur, humanitarian
b. Oct 1, 1949 Guilin, Guangxi Province, China

Nora Kaye: Ballerina, *American Ballet Theatre*
b. Jan 17, 1920 Brooklyn NY
d. Feb 28, 1987 Los Angeles CA

Helen Keller: Blind and deaf author and reformer
b. Jun 27, 1880 Tuscumbia AL
d. Jun 1, 1968 Westport CT

Billie Jean King: Tennis Champion
b. Nov 22, 1943 Long Beach CA

Eleanor King: Modern ballet dancer, *Humphrey-Weidman
Company*
b. Feb 8, 1906 Middleton PA
d. Feb 27, 1991 New York, NY

Pauline Koner: Dancer; choreographer, modern ballet
b. Jun 26, 1912 New York NY
d. Feb 8, 2001 New York NY
(Married to Fritz Mahler; see his entry)

Viola Cady Krahn: Hall of Fame diving champion, 17 world
titles, lived to be 102
b. 1902 AZ
d. Jun 1, 2004 Orange County CA

Ruth Krauss: Author of children's books, *The Carrot Seed*
b. Jul 25, 1901 Baltimore MD
d. Jul 10, 1993 Westport CT

Amalia Kussner: Artist, miniature portraits
b. Mar 26, 1863 Crawfordville IN
d. 1932 Montreux, Switzerland

Selma Lagerlof: Author, Nobel Prize for Literature, 1909
Sweden
b. Nov 20, 1858 Marbacka, Sweden
d. Mar 16, 1940 Marbacka, Sweden

Frances Langford: Singer, actress, signature song, *I'm in the Mood for Love*
b. Apr 4, 1913 Lakeland FL
d. Jul 11, 2005 Jensen Beach FL

Maria Lassnig: Austrian artist, avant-garde human forms
b. Sep 8, 1919 Kappel, Austria

Marie Paulze Lavoisiere: Woman scientist/chemist, coined term "oxygen"
b. Jan 20, 1758 Montbrison, France
d. Feb 10, 1836 Paris, France

Harper Lee: Novelist: Pulitzer Prize 1961, *To Kill a Mockingbird*
b. Apr 28, 1926 Monroeville AL

Lotte Lehmann: Opera Soprano
b. Feb 27, 1888 Perleberg, Germany
d. Aug 26, 1976 Santa Barbara CA

Frida Leider: Opera Soprano
b. Apr 18, 1888 Berlin, Germany
d. Jun 4, 1975 Berlin, Germany

Adele Leigh: Opera Soprano, London *Covent Garden Opera House*; and Vienna, and U.S.
b. Jun 15, 1928 London, England
d. May 23, 2004 London, England

Lotte Lenya: Singer-actress
b. Oct 18, 1898 Vienna, Austria
d. Nov 27, 1981 New York NY
(Wife of composer Kurt Weill)

Olga Lepeshinskaya: Prima Ballerina, *Bolshoi Ballet*
b. Sep 15, 1916 Kiev, Russia
d. Dec 20, 2008 Moscow, Russia

Rita Levi-Montalcini: Nobel Prize for Physiology/Medicine 1986, Italy

b. Apr 22, 1909 Turin, Italy
d. Dec 30, 2012 Rome, Italy

Juliette Gordon Low: Founder of the *Girl Scouts of America*
b. Oct 31, 1860 Savannah GA
d. Jan 17, 1927 Savannah GA

Myrna Loy: Actress, *The Thin Man* series
b. Aug 2, 1905 Radersburg MT
d. Dec 14, 1993 New York NY

Jeanette MacDonald: Singer of light opera; Hollywood film
    actress
b. Jun 18, 1903 Philadelphia PA
d. Jan 14, 1965 Houston TX

Lia Manoliu: 1968 Olympic gold medalist, discus thrower; 3
    medals in 6 Olympics
b. Apr 25, 1932 Chisinau, Republic of Moldova
d. Jan 9, 1998 Bucharest, Romania

Katherine Mansfield: Author, short stories
b. Oct 14, 1888 Thorndon, Wellington, New Zealand
d. Jan 9, 1923 Fountainebleau, France

Dame Alicia Markova: Ballerina
b. Dec 1, 1910 London, England
d. Dec 2, 2004 Bath, England
Agnes Martin: Artist, abstract expressionism
b. Mar 22, 1912 Macklin, Saskatchewan, Canada
d. Dec 16, 2004 Taos NM

Burnita Shelton Matthews: First woman appointed to a
    Federal District Court
b. Dec 28, 1894 Hazlehurst MS
d. Apr 25, 1988 Washington D. C.

Ekaterina Maximova: Ballerina
b. Feb 1, 1939 Moscow, Soviet Union
d. Apr 27, 2009 Moscow, Russia

Barbara McClintock: Scientist; Nobel Prize for Physiology/
Medicine 1983, US
b. Jun 16, 1902 Hartford CT
d. Sep 2, 1992 Huntington NY

Colleen McCullough: Novelist, *The Thornbirds*
b. Jun 1, 1937 Wellington, Australia

Lise Meitner: Physicist, co-discoverer of nuclear fission
b. Nov 17, 1878 Vienna, Austria
d. Oct 27, 1968 Cambridge, England

Zinka Milanov: Opera Soprano
b. May 17, 1906 Zagreb, Austria-Hungary
d. May 30, 1989 New York NY

Edna St. Vincent Millay: First woman to receive Pulitzer
Prize for Poetry, 1923
b. Feb 22, 1892 Rockland ME
d. Oct 19, 1950 Austerlitz NY

Carmen Miranda: Famous Entertainer, North and South
America
b. Feb 9, 1909 Marco de Canaveses Portugal
d. Aug 4, 1955 Beverly Hills CA

Helen Mirren: Academy Award winning actress
b. Jul 26, 1945 London, England

Gabriela Mistral: Poet; Nobel Prize for Literature 1945
b. Apr 7, 1889 Vicuna Chile
d. Jan 10, 1957 Hempstead NY

Margaret Mitchell: Author, Pulitzer Prize 1937, *Gone With the
Wind*
b. Nov 8, 1900 Atlanta GA
d. Aug 16, 1949 Atlanta GA

Lola Montes: Flamenco dancer
b. Feb 5, 1918 New York NY
d. May 16, 2008 Laguna Woods CA

Helen Wills Moody: Tennis Int'l Hall of Fame, Olympic
  gold medalist, artist, writer
b. Oct 6, 1905 Centerville (now Fremont) CA
d. Jan 1, 1998 Carmel CA

Grace Moore: Soprano in opera, musical theatre, films
b. Dec 5, 1898 Slabtown TN
d. Jan 26, 1947 near Copenhagen, Denmark

Vicki Moore: Co-founder of *Fight Against Animal Cruelty in
  Europe*
b. Dec 24, 1956 Weston Favell, Northamptonshire, England
d. Feb 6, 2000 Liverpool, England

Mourning Dove: Native American author: *Cogewea the Half-
  Blood; Tales of the Okanogans*; autobiography
b. 1888 near Bonners Ferry ID
d. Aug 8, 1936 Medical Lake WA

Jean Muir: English fashion designer
b. Jul 17, 1928 London, England
d. May 28, 1995 London, England

Iris Murdoch: Novelist
b. Jul 15, 1919 Dublin, Ireland
d. Feb 8, 1999 Oxford, England

Nadia Nerina: Ballerina with *London Royal Ballet*
b. Oct 21, 1927 Bloemfontein, South Africa
d. Oct 6, 2008 Beaulieu-sur-Mer, France

Dika Newlin: Child Prodigee, composed opera, chamber
  music; later music professor and rock performer
b. Nov 22, 1923 Portland OR
d. Jul 22, 2006 Richmond VA

Inga Nielsen: Opera soprano
b. Jun 2, 1946 Copenhagen, Denmark
d. Feb 10, 2008 Copenhagen, Denmark

Florence Nightingale: Founder of modern nursing
b. May 12, 1820 Florence, Italy

d. Aug 13, 1910 London, England

Birgit Nilsson: Opera soprano
b. May 17, 1918 Vastra Karup, Sweden
d. Dec 25, 2005 Vastra Karup, Sweden

Emmy Noether: Prominent mathematician
b. Mar 23, 1882 Erlangen, Germany
d. Apr 14, 1935 Bryn Mawr PA

Lillian Nordica: Opera soprano
b. Dec 12, 1857 Farmington ME
d. May 10, 1914 Island of Java

Christiane Nüsslein-Volhard, shared Nobel Prize for Physi-
ology/Medicine 1995, Germany
b. Oct 20, 1942 Magdeburg, Germany

Annie Oakley: Legendary sharpshooter
b. Aug 13, 1860 Darke County OH
d. Nov 3, 1926 Greenville OH

Joyce Carol Oates: Novelist, playwright, literary critic
b. Jun 16, 1938 Lockport NY

Anita O'Day: Singer, big band and jazz
b. Oct 18, 1919 Chicago IL
d. Nov 23, 2006 Los Angeles CA

Georgia O'Keeffe: American artist, painter
b. Nov 15, 1887 Sun Prairie WI
d. Mar 6, 1986 Santa Fe NM

Rose O'Neill: Illustrator, artist, writer, invented the *Kewpie
Doll*
b. Jun 25, 1874 Wilkes-Barre PA
d. Apr 6, 1944 Ozark MO

Maureen Orcutt: Golf champion, two USGA championships, won more than 65 major tournaments
b. Apr 1, 1907 New York NY
d. Jan 9, 2007 Durham, NC

Elinor Awan Ostrom: Only woman to win Nobel Prize for
    Economics, 2009, US
b. Aug. 7, 1933 Los Angeles CA
d. Jun 12, 2012 Bloomington, IN

Ruth Packer: Opera soprano, *Royal Opera House, Sadler Wells
    Opera*
b. Oct 22, 1910 London, England
d. Jan 12, 2005 Sao Bras de Alportel, Portugal

Ruth Page, Dancer-choreographer, founded *Chicago Opera
    Ballet*
b. Mar 22, 1899 Indianapolis IN
d. Apr 7, 1991 Chicago IL

Dorothy Parker: Short story writer, poet
b. Aug 22, 1893 West End NJ
d. Jun 7, 1967 NewYork NY

Rosa Parks: Civil rights activist
b. Feb 4, 1913 Tuskegee AL
d. Oct 24, 2005 Detroit MI

Mary L. Parr: lived to be 113
b. Feb 1, 1889 IN
d. Oct 29, 2002 FL

Adelina Patti: Opera soprano
b. Feb 19, 1843 Madrid, Spain
d. Sep 27, 1919 Craig-y-Nos Brecknockshire, Wales

Alice Stokes Paul: Founded *National Women's Party*
b. Jan 11, 1885 Moorestown NJ
d. Jul 9, 1977 Moorestown NJ

Michelle Paver: Author: Novelist; children's books, *Wolf
    Brother, Spirit Walker*
b. 1960 Malawi, Africa

Anna Pavlova: Russian ballet dancer
b. Jan 31/Feb 12 1881 St. Petersburg, Russia

d. Jan 23 1931 Hague, Netherlands

Ethel Payne: American Journalist "First Lady of the Black
    Press"
b. Aug 14, 1911 Chicago IL
d. May 28, 1991 Washington D. C.

Minnie Pearl (a.k.a. Sarah Colley): Comedienne
b. Oct 25, 1912 Centerville TN
d. Mar 4, 1996 Nashville TN

Phoebe Pember: Confederate nurse; published memoirs;
    honored on US postage stamp
b. Aug 18, 1823 Charleston SC
d. Mar 4, 1913 Pittsburgh PA

Evita (Eva) Perón: First Lady of Argentina and social re-
    former, "Spiritual Leader of the Nation"
b. May 7, 1919 Los Toldos, Argentina
d. Jul 26, 1952 Buenos Aires, Argentina

Marta Perez: International opera mezzo-soprano
b. Aug 2, 1924 Havana, Cuba
d. Aug 18, 2009 Miami FL

Bernadette Peters: Singer, actress, benefits for animal
    welfare
b. Feb 28, 1948 New York NY

Suzanne Pleshette: Actress, films and television
b. Jan 31, 1937 New York NY
d. Jan 19, 2008 Los Angleles CA

Maya Plisetskaya: Prima ballerina
b. Nov 20, 1925 Moscow, Russia

Lily Pons: Opera soprano
b. Apr 12, 1898 Draguignan, France
d. Feb 13, 1976 Dallas TX

Rosa Ponselle: Opera soprano
b. Jan 22, 1897 Meriden CT

d. May 25, 1981 near Baltimore MD

Beatrix Potter: Author of children's books, *Peter Rabbit*
b. Jul 28, 1866 London, England
d. Dec 22, 1943 Lancashire, England

Leontyne Price: Opera soprano
b. Feb 10, 1027 Laurel MS

Harriet Quimby: Pioneer aviator, first American woman to
    earn a pilot's license and pilot the English Channel.
b. May 11, 1875, Arcadia, MI
d. Jul 1, 1912 Squantum MA

Ann Radcliffe: Pioneered the Gothic novel, *The Castles of Athlin and Dunbayne*
b. Jul 9, 1764 London, England
d. Feb 7, 1823 London, England

Gilda Radner: Comedienne
b. Jun 28, 1946 Detroit MI
d. May 20, 1989 Los Angeles CA

Ayn Rand: Novelist, *Fountainhead, Atlas Shrugged*; philosopher:
    Objectivism
b. Feb 2, 1905 St. Petersburg, Russia
d. Mar 6, 1982 New York City NY

Jeannette Rankin: First US Congresswoman
b. Jun 11, 1880 Missoula Co. MT
d. May 18, 1973 Carmel CA

Nell Rankin: Opera mezzo-soprano, NY *Metropolitan Opera*
b. Jan 3, 1924 Montgomery AL
d. Jan 13, 2005 New York NY

Marjorie Kinnan Rawlings: Author, *The Yearling*, Pulitzer
    Prize
b. Aug 8, 1896 Washington DC
d. Dec 14, 1953 St. Augustine FL

Anne Revere: Actress, Broadway (Tony winner); Hollywood (3 Oscar nominations)
b. Jun 25, 1903 New York NY
d. Dec 18, 1990 Locust Valley NY

Condoleezza Rice: US Secretary of State
b. Nov 14, 1954 Birmingham AL

Sally Ride: Astronaut
b. May 26, 1951 Encino CA

Amalia Rodrigues: Popular singing star
b. Jul 23, 1920 Lisbon, Portugal
d. Oct 6, 1999 Lisbon, Portugal

Ginger Rogers: Film dancer, actress
b. Jul 16, 1911 Independence MO
d. Apr 25, 1995 Rancho Mirage CA

Ernestine Rose: Abolitionist, suffragist; co-founder of *Assoc.
of All Classes, All Nations*
b. Jan 13, 1810 Piotrkow, Poland
d. Aug 4, 1892 Brighton, East Sussex, England

Nelly Sachs: Poet, Nobel Prize for Literature, 1966 Sweden
b. Dec 10, 1891 Berlin, Germany
d. May 12, 1970 Stockholm, Sweden

Jessica Savage: Television broadcaster and news reporter
b. Feb 1, 1947 Kennett Square PA
d. Oct 23, 1983 New Hope PA

Diane Sawyer: Television journalist, newswoman, political
correspondent,
b. Dec 22, 1945 Glasgow KY

Josephine Schwartz: Choreographer, founder of *Dayton Ballet Co.*
b. Apr 8, 1908 Dayton OH
d. Feb 27, 2004 Boulder CO

Dame Elisabeth Schwarzkopf: Opera soprano

b. Dec 9, 1915 Jarotschin, Prussia (now Poland)
d. Aug 3, 2006 Vorarlberg, Austria

Amalie Seckbach: Painter, sculptress
b. May 7, 1870 near Frankfurt, Germany
d. Aug 10, 1944 Terezin, Czechoslovakia, concentration
   camp

Dr. Vandana Shiva: Physicist, Ecologist
b. Nov 5, 1952 Dehra Dun, India

Margaret 'Lionel' Shriver: Author of *We Need to Talk About
   Kevin*
b. May 18, 1957 Gastonia NC

Carol Houck Smith: V.P. and editor-at-large of W.W. Norton & Co. book publisher
b. 1923 Buffalo NY
d. Nov 29, 2008 New York NY

Ethel Smith: Organist "First Lady of the Hammond Organ"
b. Nov 22, 1902 Pittsburgh PA
d. May 10, 1996 Palm Beach FL

Joan Smith: Novelist and journalist, *What Will Survive*
b. Aug 27, 1953 London, England

Kate Smith: Popular singer
b. May 1, 1909 Greenville VA
d. Jun 17, 1986 Raleigh NC

Margaret Chase Smith: US Congresswoman; US Senator
b. Dec 14, 1897 Skowhegan ME
d. May 29, 1995 Skowhegan ME

Dame Ethel Smyth: Composer of choral music, symphonies
   and operas; suffragist
b. Apr 23, 1858 London, England
d. May 8, 1944 Woking, England

Sonia Sotomayor: U.S. Supreme Court Justice
b. Jun 25, 1954 The Bronx NY

Phyllis Spira: South Africa's prima ballerina; performed
with *London Royal Ballet*
b. Oct 18 1943 Johannesburg, South Africa
d. Mar 11, 2008 Cape Town, South Africa

Ruth St. Denis: Dancer-choreographer, modern ballet
b. Jan 20, 1878 Newark NJ
d. Jul 21, 1968 Los Angeles CA

Gloria Steinem: Journalist; editor, *Ms. Magazine*
b. Mar 25, 1934 Toledo OH

Helen Stephens: Olympic sprinter, 2 gold medals 1936
b. Feb 3, 1918 Fulton MO
d. Jan 17, 1994 St. Louis MO

Dorothy Stone: Virtuoso flutist, composer
b. Jun 7, 1958 Kingston PA
d. Mar 7, 2008 Green Valley CA

Lily Strickland: Composer, artist, writer
b. 1884 Anderson Co. SC
d. Jun 6, 1958 Hendersonville NC

Guilhermina Suggia: Famous woman cellist
b. 1885 Oporto, Portugal
d. 1950 Oporto, Portugal

Anne Sullivan: Helen Keller's teacher and friend
b. Apr 14, 1866 Feeding Hills MA
d. Oct 20, 1936 Forest Hills NY

Wislawa Szymborska: Poet, Essayist, Nobel Prize for Literature 1996, Poland
b. Jul 2, 1923 Prowent, Poland
d. Feb 1, 2012 Kraków, Poland

Magdalena Tagliaferro: Critically-acclaimed classical pianist, played into her nineties
b. Jan 19, 1893 Rio de Janeiro, Brazil
d. Sep 9, 1986 Rio de Janeiro, Brazil

Ida M. Tarbell: Biographer, historian
b. Nov 5, 1857 Erie County PA
d. Jan 6, 1944 Bridgeport CT

Holland Taylor: Actress, theatre, television and films
b. Jan 14, 1943 Philadelphia PA

June Taylor: Choreographer, June Taylor Dancers, *Jackie
    Gleason Show*
b. Dec 14, 1917 Chicago IL
d. May 16, 2004 Miami FL

Renata Tebaldi: Opera singer
b. Feb 1, 1922 Pesaro, Italy
d. Dec 19, 2004 San Marino, Italy

Fay Templeton: Broadway star, light opera
b. Dec 25, 1865, Little Rock, Arkansas
d. Oct 3, 1939, San Francisco, California

Mother Teresa: Catholic saint; Nobel Peace Prize 1979, India
b. Aug 27, 1910 Skopje, Macedonia
d. Sep 5, 1997 Calcutta, India

Sister Rosetta Tharpe: Celebrity gospel singer of the 40s
    and 50s
b. Mar 20, 1915 Cotton Plant AR
d. Oct 9, 1973 Philadelphia PA

Kay Thompson: Entertainer, author of children's
    books, *Eloise*
b. Nov 9, 1902 St. Louis MO
d. Jul 2, 1998 Manhattan NY

May Esther Peterson Thompson: Opera soprano
b. Oct 7, 1880 Oshkosh WI
d. Oct 8, 1952 Austin TX

Tamara Toumanova: Russian-born American ballerina
b. Mar 2, 1919 Tyumen, Siberia, Russia
d. May 29, 1996 Santa Monica CA

Jennie Tourel: Opera mezzo-soprano
b. Jun 22/26, 1900 Vitebsk, Russia
d. Nov 23, 1973 New York, NY

Dorothy Townsend: First woman to cover local news for *LA Times*, 1966 Pulitzer Prize for coverage of Watts riots
b. Feb 25, 1924 Claude TX
d. Mar 5, 2012 Sherman Oaks CA

Myrtle Tremblay: Watercolor artist
b. Dec 9, 1908, Albion, MI
d. Sep 3, 2011 New Holland PA

Harriet Tubman: Escaped slave who helped free others
b. 1820? Bucktown, Dorchester County MD
d. Mar 10, 1913 Auburn NY

Elizabeth Tudor: Queen Elizabeth I of England
b. Sep 7, 1533 Greenwich Palace, England
d. Mar 24, 1603 Richmond Palace, England

Dame Eva Turner: Opera soprano
b. Mar 10, 1892 Werneth, Oldham, England
d. Jun 16, 1990 London, England

Mitsuko Uchida: Internationally acclaimed classical pianist
b. Dec 20, 1948 Tokyo, Japan

Galina Ulanova: Russian prima ballerina
b. Jan 8, 1910 St. Petersburg, Russia
d. Mar 21, 1998 Moscow, Russia

Ninette de Valois: Founder, *London Royal Ballet*
b. Jun 6, 1898 County Wicklow, Ireland
d. Mar 8, 2001 London, England

Mrs. Hendrikje 'Hennie' Van Andel-Schipper: Lived to be 115 with good memory
b. Jun 29, 1890 Smilde, Netherlands
d. Aug 30, 2005 Hoogeveen, Netherlands

Carol Vaness: International opera soprano
b. Jul 27, 1952 San Diego CA

Astrid Varnay: Opera soprano
b. Apr 25, 1918 Stockholm, Sweden
d. Sep 4, 2006 Munich, Germany

Kyra Vayne: Opera soprano
b. Jan 29, 1916 Petrograd, Russia
d. Jan 12, 2001 London, England

Elizabeth Janet (Gray) Vining: Novels, and children's books
b. Oct 6, 1902 Philadelphia PA
d. Nov 27, 1999 Longwood PA

Bertha von Suttner: Author, *Lay Down Your Arms!*, Nobel
Peace Prize, 1905
b. Jun 9, 1843 Prague, Austrian Empire
d. Jun 21, 1914 Vienna, Austria

Thelma Votipka: Opera singer, supporting roles, 1,422 per-
formances, *Metropolitan Opera*
b. Dec 20, 1898 Cleveland OH
d. Oct 24, 1972 New York NY

Grete Waitz: Marathon runner, Olympics silver medal,
World Championships gold medal, won nine NYC
Marathons,
b. Oct 1, 1953 Oslo, Norway
d. Apr 19, 2011 Oslo, Norway

Nancy Wake: WWII Decorated spy for the Allies
b. Aug 30, 1912 Wellington, New Zealand
d. Aug 11, 2011 London, England, UK

Cindy Walker: Country Music Hall of Fame songwriter
b. Jul 20, 1918 Mart TX
d. Mar 23, 2006 Mexia TX

Dr. Mary Walker: Civil War doctor; advocated reform in
women's fashions
b. Nov 26, 1832 Oswego NY

d. Feb 21, 1919 Oswego NY

Ganna Walska: Landscape artist, *Lotusland*
b. 1887 Brest-Litovsk, Poland
d. Mar 2, 1984 Lotusland, CA

Ethel Waters: Blues and jazz singer; actress
b. Oct 31, 1896 Chester PA
d. Sep 1, 1977 Chatsworth CA

Mae West: Movie Actress
b. Aug 17, 1893 Brooklyn NY
d. Nov 22, 1980 Los Angeles CA

Edith Wharton: Novelist: *The House of Mirth, Age of Inno-cence,* Pulitzer Prize 1921
b. Jan 24, 1862 New York NY
d. Aug 11, 1937 near Paris, France

Willye White: Olympic silver medalist in track and field
b. Dec. 31, 1939, in Money MS
d. Feb 6, 2007 Chicago IL

Camilla Williams: First Afro-American opera soprano
b. Oct 18, 1919 Danville VA
d. Jan 29, 1912 Bloomington IN

Mary Lou Williams: Jazz musician and composer
b. May 8, 1910 Atlanta GA
d. May 28, 1981 Durham NC

Frances E. Willard: Educator, temperance leader, feminist
b. Sep 28, 1839 Churchville NY
d. Feb 17, 1898 New York NY

Sallie Wilson: Principal ballet dancer, *American Ballet Theatre*
b. Apr 18, 1932 Ft. Worth TX
d. Apr 27, 2008 New York NY

Oprah Winfrey: TV talk show host
b. Jan 29, 1954 Kosciusko MS

Katarina Witt: Figure skater, 2 Olympic gold medals, 5
   world championships
b. Dec 3, 1965 Staaken, Germany

Maude Woods Wodehouse: Philanthropist
b. c1916 Huehue Kona HI
d. Jul 2, 2003 Keauhou, HI

Virginia Woolf: Writer of novels, essays
b. Jan 25, 1882 London, England
d. Mar 28, 1941 Sussex, England

Katharine Wright: Aviator, "The Third Wright Brother"
b. Aug 19, 1874 Dayton OH
d. Mar 3, 1926 Kansas City

Berta Yampolsky: Co-founder and artistic director of *Israel
   Ballet Company*
b. Feb 7, 1934 Paris, France

Marguerite Young: Novelist, historian, *Miss MacIntosh, My
   Darling*
b. Aug 28, 1908 Indianapolis IN
d. Nov 17, 1995 Indianapolis IN

Safiya (a.k.a. Safiyya) Zaghloul: Egyptian pioneer feminist;
   challenged British occupation
b. Jun 16, 1876 Cairo, Egypt
d. Jan 12, 1946 Egypt

Mildred 'Babe' Didrikson Zaharias: Olympic Gold medalist;
   versatile athlete
b. Jun 26, 1911/14 Port Arthur TX
d. Sep 27, 1956 Galveston TX

Table 2: Famous Men Who Didn't Have Children

Charles Greely Abbot: Astrophysicist, devised measurement of solar radiation
b. May 31, 1872 Wilton NH
d. Dec 17, 1973 Riverdale MD

Forrest J Ackerman: Sci-Fi writer and promoter who coined
the term "Sci-Fi"
b. Nov 24, 1916 Los Angeles CA
d. Dec 5, 2008 Los Angeles CA

Charles Addams: Cartoonist: The Addams Family
b. Jan 7, 1912 Westfield, NJ
d. Sep 29, 1988 New York NY

Robert Adler: Physicist for Zenith, co-inventor of TV re-
mote control
b. Dec 4, 1913 Vienna, Austria
d. Feb 15, 2007 Boise ID

Alvin Ailey: Dancer, choreographer, *Alvin Ailey American
Dance Theatre*
Jan 5, 1931 Rogers TX
d. Dec 1, 1989 New York NY

Vicente Aleixandre: Poet, Nobel Prize for literature 1977
b. Apr 26, 1898 Seville, Spain
d. Dec 14, 1984 near Madrid, Spain

Hans Christian Andersen: Author of children's stories
b. Apr 2, 1805 Odense, Denmark
d. Aug 4, 1875 Copenhagen, Denmark

Ivo Andric: Nobel Prize for Literature 1961 Yugoslavia
b. Oct 9, 1892 Dolac, Bosnia and Herzegovina
d. Mar 13, 1975 Belgrade, Belgrade, Yugoslavia

Sir Norman Angell: Nobel Prize for Peace 1933 UK
b. Dec 26, 1872 Holbeach, England
d. Oct 7, 1967 London, England

Michelangelo Antonioni: Filmmaker, Oscar for lifetime
achievement
b. Sep 29, 1912 Ferrara, Italy
d. Jul 30, 2007 Rome, Italy

Jules Francois Archibald: Australian Journalist
b. Jan 14, 1856 Kildare, Victoria, Australia
d. Sep 10, 1919 Sydney, Australia

Edwin Yancey (a.k.a. Yancy) Argo: Member of first U.S.
Olympic team to win gold medal in equestrian events
b. Sep 22, 1895 in Hollins AL
d. Mar 10, 1962 Shreveport, LA

Giorgio Armani: Fashion designer
b. Jul 11, 1934 Piacenza, Italy

Francis William Aston: Nobel Prize for Chemistry 1922 UK
b. Sep 1, 1877 Harborne, Birmingham, England
d. Nov 20, 1945 Cambridge, England

Dr. Robert Atkins: Diet guru
b. Oct 17, 1930 Columbus OH
d. Apr 17, 2003 New York NY

Gene Autry: Singing cowboy
b. Sep 29, 1907 Tioga TX
d. Oct 2, 1998 Studio City CA

Francis Bacon: Philosopher
b. Jan 22, 1561 London, England
d. Apr 9, 1626 London, England

Dan Bain: Ice hockey (Hall of Fame 1949), figure skating,
gymnastics, cycling championships
b. Feb 14, 1874 Belleville, Ontario, Canada
d. Aug 15, 1962 Winnipeg, Manitoba, Canada

Mily Balakirev: Classical composer, conductor
b. Jan 2, 1837 Nizhny Novgorod, Russia
d. May 29, 1910, St Petersburg

George Balanchine: Choreographer
b. Jan 22, 1904 St. Petersburg, Russia
d. Apr 30, 1983 New York NY

Samuel Barber: Composer, opera, orchestral, chamber, Pulitzer Prize winner
b. Mar 9, 1910 Westchester PA
d. Jan 23, 1981 New York NY

Sir John Barbirolli: Renowned conductor, NY *Philharmonic* and *Hallé Orchestras*
b. Dec 2, 1899 London, England
d. Jul 29, 1970 London, England

Bob Barker: Long time TV host
b. Dec 12, 1923 Darrington WA

Howard Barlow: Radio; CBS music director; NBC conductor *Voice of Firestone*
b. May 1, 1892 Plain City OH
d. Jan 31, 1972 Danbury CT

J.M. Barrie: Playwright, author of *Peter Pan*
b. May 9, 1860 Kirriemuir, Scotland
d. Jun 19, 1937 London, England

Robert Abram Bartlett: Arctic explorer, first to sail north of 88 degrees N. Latitude
b. Aug 15, 1875 Brigus, Newfoundland
d. Apr 28, 1946 New York NY

James A. Beard: Renowned chef, TV and books
b. May 5, 1903 Portland OR
d. Jan 23, 1985 New York NY

Samuel Beckett: Poet, playwright; Nobel Prize for literature 1969
b. Apr 13, 1906 Dublin, Ireland
d. Dec 22, 1989 Paris, France

William Beebe: Naturalist, oceanographer, ornithologist
b. Jul 29, 1877 Brooklyn NY

d. Jun 4, 1962 Simla, Trinidad West Indies

Ludwig van Beethoven: Composer
b. Dec 16, 1770 Bonn, Germany
d. Mar 26, 1827 Vienna, Austria

Maurice Bejart: Choreographer
b. Jan 1, 1927 Marseille, France
d. Nov 22, 2007 Lausanne, Switzerland

Georg von Bekesy: Nobel Prize for Physiology/Medicine
    1961 US
b. Jun 3, 1899 Budapest, Hungary
d. Jun 13, 1972 Honolulu HI

Vincenzo Bellini: Classical composer
b. Nov 3: 1801 Catania, Sicily
d. Sep 23, 1836 Paris, France

Jacinto Benavente: Nobel Prize for Literature 1922 Spain
b. Aug 12, 1866 Madrid, Spain
d. Jul 14, 1954 Madrid, Spain

Jeremy Bentham: Philosopher (on politics and morality)
b. Feb 15, 1748 London, England
d. Jun 6, 1832 London, England

Jean Béraud: French Impressionist painter
b. Jan 12, 1849 Saint Petersburg, Russia
d. Oct 4, 1935 Paris, France

Irénée Marius Bergé: Composed classical suites, choral can-
    tatas, music for silent films
b. Feb 1, 1867 Toulouse, France
d. Jul 30, 1926 Jersey City NJ

Kristian Olaf Bernhard Birkeland: Physicist; 7 Nobel Prize
    nominations
b. Dec 13, 1867 Oslo, Norway
d. Jun 15, 1917 Tokyo, Japan

Olav Olavson Bjaaland: Polar explorer with first group to
   reach South Pole, champion skier: Holmenkollen medal
b. Mar 5, 1873 Morgedal, Norway
d. Jun 8, 1961 Norway

Eubie Blake: Composer and pianist, ragtime and jazz
b. Feb 7, 1883 Baltimore MD
d. Feb 12, 1983 Brooklyn NY

William Blake: Artist, engraver, poet
b. Nov 28, 1757 London, England
d. Aug 12, 1827 London, England

Marc Blitzstein: Theatre composer. *The Cradle Will Rock*
b. Mar 2, 1905 Philadelphia PA
d. Jan 22, 1964 Martinique Island, Caribbean Sea

Ray Bolger: Actor, entertainer, *Scarecrow in Wizard of Oz*
b. Jan 10, 1904 Boston MA
d. Jan 15, 1987 Los Angeles CA

Charles Joseph Bonaparte: US Attorney-General under
   Teddy Roosevelt; founded FBI
b. Jun 9, 1851 Baltimore MD
d. Jun 28, 1921 Baltimore MD

Edouard Borovansky: Ballet director, *Borovansky Ballet*,
   Australia
b. Feb 24, 1902 Prerov, Czech Republic
d. Dec 18, 1959 Randwick, Australia

Roberto Bracco: Dramatist, novelist, Nobel Prize nominee
b. Nov 10, 1861 Naples, Italy
d. Apr 20, 1943 Sorrento, Italy

Ed Bradley: TV news journalist, CBS News, *60 Minutes*
b. Jun 22, 1941 Philadelphia PA'd.
d. Nov 9, 2006 New York NY

Johannes Brahms: Composer
b. May 7, 1833 Hamburg, Germany
d. Apr 3, 1897 Vienna, Austria

Aristide Briand: French Prime Minister; Nobel Peace Prize, 1926
b. Mar 28, 1862 Nantes, France
d. Mar 7, 1932 Paris, France

Benjamin Britten: Composer, conductor:
b. Nov 22, 1913 Lowestoft, Suffolk, England
d. Dec 4, 1976 Aldeburgh, Suffolk, England

Louis de Broglie: Nobel Prize for Physics 1929 France
b. Aug 16, 1892 Dieppe, France
d. Mar 19, 1987 Louveciennes, France

Anton Bruckner: Classical composer
b. Sep 4, 1824 Ansfelden, Austria
d. Oct 11, 1896 Vienna, Austria

Erik Bruhn: International ballet Star
b. Oct 3, 1928 Copenhagen, Denmark
d. Apr 1, 1986 Toronto, Ontario, Canada

James Buchanan: President of the United States
b. Apr 23, 1791 Franklin County, PA
d. Jun 1, 1868 Lancaster PA

James McGill Buchanan: Nobel Prize for Economics 1986 US
b. Oct 2, 1919 Murfreesboro TN

Russell Alexander Buchanan: WWI & WWII vet, lived to be 106, still mentally alert
b. Jan 24, 1900 MA?
d. Dec 6, 2006 Cambridge MA

Mikhail Bulgakov: Satirist, novelist, playwright
b. May 3/15, 1891 Kiev, Ukraine
d. Mar 10, 1940 Moscow, Russia

Revol Samoilovich Bunin: Composed symphonies, sonatas, movie scores
b. Apr 6, 1924 Moscow, Russia
d. Jul 3, 1976 Moscow, Russia

Michelangelo Buonarroti: painter, sculptor
b. Mar 6, 1475 Caprese, Italy
d. Feb 18, 1564 Rome, Italy

Luther Burbank: Horticulturist, botanist, pioneer in agricultural science
b. Mar 7, 1849 Lancaster MA
d. Apr 11, 1926 Santa Rosa CA

Ernie Bushmiller: Cartoonist, *Fritzi Ritz*, and the long running *Nancy* comic strip
b. Aug 23, 1905 New York NY
d. Aug 15, 1982 Stamford CT

Reuben Bussey: Artist, oils, watercolors, sketches, portraits and landscapes
b. Feb 12, 1818 Nottingham, England
d. Mar 1, 1893 Nottingham, England

Alfred Mosher Butts: Architect, and inventor of the Scrabble game
b. Apr 13, 1899 Poughkeepsie
d. Apr 4, 1993 Rhinebeck NY

John Cage: Composer of avant garde music
b. Sep 5, 1912 Los Angeles CA
d. Aug 12, 1992 Manhattan NY

James Cain: Journalist, novelist, crime writer
b. Jul 1, 1892 Annapolis MD
d. Oct 27, 1977 University Park, MD

Salvatore Capezio: Founder of Capezio ballet shoes
b. Apr 13, 1871 Muro Lucano, Italy
d. 1940 New York, NY?

Benjamin N. Cardozo: U.S. Supreme Court Justice, 1932 until his death
b. May 24, 1870 New York NY
d. Jul 9, 1938 Port Chester NY

Alexis Carrel: Nobel Prize for Physiology/Medicine 1912
France
b. Jun 28, 1873 Sainte-Foy-les-Lyon, France
d. Nov 5, 1944 Paris, France

Lewis Carroll (a.k.a. Charles L. Dodson); Author *Alice's Adventures in Wonderland*
b. Jan 27, 1832 Daresbury, England
d. Jan 14, 1898 Guilford, England

John Cartwright: British reformer who favored American independence from England
b. Sep 17, 1740 Marnham, Nottinghamshire, England
d. Sep 23, 1824 London, England

George Washington Carver: Inventor, scientist, educator; hundreds of uses of peanuts
b. Jul 12, 1864? near Diamond Grove MO
d. Jan 5, 1943 Tuskegee AL

Pablo Casals: Cellist
b. Dec 29, 1876 Vendrell, Spain
d. Oct 22, 1973 San Juan, Puerto Rico

Jim E. Casey: Founded United Parcel Service
b. Mar 29, 1888 Pick Handle Gulch NV
d. Jun 6, 1983 Seattle WA

Henry Cavendish: Physicist and chemist, discovered hydrogen
b. Oct 10, 1731 Nice, France
d. Feb 24, 1810 London, England

Robert Cecil: Nobel Prize for Peace 1937 UK
b. Sep 14, 1864 London, England
d. Nov 24, 1958 Tunbridge Wells, Kent, England

Subrahmanyan Chandrasekhar: Nobel Prize for Physics 1983 US
b. Oct 19, 1910 Lahore, India (now Pakistan)
d. Aug 21, 1995 Chicago IL

Anton Chekhov: Russian Playwright
b. Jan 29, 1860 Taganrog, Russia
d. Jul 14–15, 1904 Badenweiler, Germany

Nicholas Chevalier: Artist: painter, lithographer, Australia
    and Europe
b. May 9, 1828 St. Petersburg, Russia
d. Mar 15, 1902 London, England

Frederic Chopin: Composer; pianist
b. Feb 22/Mar 1 1810 Zelazowa, Poland
d. Oct 17, 1849 Paris, France

Arthur C. Clarke: Sci-fi author: *2001: A Space Odyssey*
b. Dec 16, 1917 Minehead, England
d. Mar 19, 2008 Sri Lanka

George Clooney: Movie actor
b. May 6, 1961 Lexington KY

Nicolaus Copernicus: Astronomer, Astrologer, argued a he-
    liocentric solar system
b. 1473 Torun, Poland
d. 1543 Frombork, Poland

Aaron Copland: American composer
b. Nov 14, 1900 New York NY
d. Dec 2, 1990 New York NY

Harry E. Cooper: World Golf Hall of Fame, numerous
    championships
b. Aug 6, 1904 Leatherhead, England
d. Oct 17, 2000 White Plains, New York

Jim Corbett: World champion heavyweight boxer
b. Sep 1, 1866 San Francisco CA
d. Feb 18, 1933 New York NY

Arcangelo Corelli: Composer of Baroque music, violinist
b. Feb 17, 1653 Fusignano, Italy
d. Jan 8, 1713 Rome, Italy

Franco Corelli: Opera tenor
b. Apr 8, 1921 Ancona, Italy
d. Oct 29, 2003 Milan, Italy

Louis Marie-Anne Couperus: Dutch novelist and poet
b. Jun 10 1863 The Hague, Netherlands
d. Jul 16, 1923 De Steeg, Netherlands

Chief Plenty Coups: The last of the Crow Chiefs
b. 1848 probably near Billings MT
d. Mar 3, 1932 MT

Del Courtney: Big Band leader, 1930s
b. Sep 21, 1910 Oakland CA
d. Feb 11, 2006 Honolulu HI

James Gould Cozzens: Novelist, 1949 Pulitzer Prize, *Guard of Honor*
b. Aug 19, 1903 Chicago IL
d. Aug 9, 1978 Stuart FL

Donald J. Cram: Nobel Prize for Chemistry 1987 US
b. Apr 22, 1919 Chester VT
d. Jun 17, 2001 Palm Desert CA

Randal Cremer: Nobel Prize for Peace 1903 UK
b. Mar 18, 1828 Fareham, England
d. Jul 22, 1908 London, England

George Cukor: Film Director
b. Jul 7, 1899 New York NY
d. Jan 24, 1983 Hollywood CA

Peter Henrik Dam: Nobel Prize for Medicine/Physiology
(vitamin K) 1943, Denmark
b. Feb 21, 1895 Copenhagen, Denmark
d. Apr 17, 1976 Copenhagen, Denmark

Mahmoud Darwish: Palestinian poet of many literary prizes
b. Mar 13, 1941 Al Birweh, Galilee
d. Aug 9, 2008 Houston TX

Leonardo Da Vinci: Artist, inventor, scientist
b. Apr 15, 1452 Vinci, Italy
d. May 2, 1519 Cloux (a.k.a. Clos Lucé), France

Peter Smith Dawson: Baritone singer, concerts; early phonograph recordings
b. Jan 31, 1882 Adelaide, Australia
d. Sep 27, 1961 Sydney, Australia

Eugene Victor Debs: Union organizer, founded *Int'l Workers
   of the Worldz*
b. Nov 5, 1855 Terre Haute IN
d. Oct 20, 1926 Elmhurst IL

Edgar Degas: Artist, French Impressionism
b. Jul 19, 1834 Paris, France
d. Sep 27, 1917 Paris, France

Manuel De Falla: Spanish composer
b. Nov 23, 1876 Cadiz, Spain
d. Nov 14, 1946 Alta Gracia, Argentina

Frederick Delius: English composer
b. Jan 29, 1862 Bradford, Yorkshire, England
d. Jun 10, 1934 Grez-sur-Loing, France

C.J. Dennis: Poetry, and children's books of poetry: 731
   poems
b. Sep 7, 1876 Auburn, South Australia
d. Jun 22, 1938 Melbourne, Australia

Antoine Deparcieux: French mathematician
b. Oct 28, 1703 Peyremale, France
d. Sep 2, 1768 Paris, France

Josquin Des Pres (a.k.a. Des Prez): Renaissance Franco-
   Flemish composer, most famous of his time
b. c1455 Conde-sur-l'Escaut, Hainaut (now
   France-Belgium)
d. Aug 27, 1521 Conde-sur-l'Escaut, Hainaut

Christian Dior: Fashion designer

b. Jan 21, 1905 Angers, France
d. Oct 23, 1957 Montecatini, Italy

Donatello (Donato di Niccolô di Betto Bardi): Sculptor
b. c1386 Florence, Italy
d. Dec 13, 1466 Florence, Italy

Archie Drake: Bass-baritone with *Seattle Opera* for 40 years
b. Mar 13, 1925 Great Yarmouth, England
d. May 24, 2006 Seattle WA

Allen Stuart Drury: Novelist, Pulitzer Prize 1960, *Advise and Consent*
b. Sep 2, 1918 Houston, TX
d. Sep 2, 1998 Tiburon, CA

Jean Henri Dunant aka Henry Dunant: Nobel Prize for Peace 1901 Switzerland
May 8, 1828 Geneva, Switzerland
Oct 30, 1910 Heiden, Switzerland

Albrecht Durer: Artist, painter, print maker, mathematician
b. May 21, 1471 Nuremberg, Germany (Holy Roman Empire)
d. Apr 6, 1528 Nuremberg, Germany

Thomas Eakins: Artist: realism, figures and portraits
b. Jul 25, 1844 Philadelphia PA
d. Jun 25, 1916 Philadelphia PA

George Eastman: (Eastman-Kodak) revolutionized photography; philanthropist
b. Jul 12, 1854 Waterville NY
d. Mar 14, 1932 Rochester NY

Roger Ebert: Film Critic, first film critic to win a Pulitzer Prize
b. Jun 18, 1942 Urbana IL
d. Apr 4, 2013 Chicago IL

T.S. Eliot: Poet, editor; Nobel Prize for Literature, 1948
b. Sep 26, 1888 St. Louis, MO
d. Jan 4, 1965 London, England

Odysseus Elytis: Poet, essayist, Nobel Prize for Literature
1979 Greece
b. Nov 2, 1911 Iráklion, Crete, Greece
d. Mar 18, 1996 Athens, Greece

Ray Evans: Hollywood lyricist, songs include Mona Lisa,
Silver Bells
b. Feb 4, 1915 Salamanca NY
d. Feb 15, 2007 Los Angeles CA

Hans Fantel: Founding editor of *Stereo Review*; columnist for
NY *Times*
b. Mar 1, 1922 Vienna, Austria
d. May 21, 2006 Springfield MA

Michael Faraday: Physicist; discovered electromagnetic
induction
b. Sep 22, 1791 Newington Butts, England
d. Aug 25, 1867 London, England

George Washington Gale Ferris: Inventor of the Ferris
Wheel
b. Feb 14, 1859 Galesburg IL
d. Nov 22, 1896 Pittsburgh PA

Ernest Otto Fischer: Nobel for Chemistry 1973 (West)
Germany
b. Nov 10, 1918 Solln, now Munich, Germany
d. Jul 23, 2007 Munich, Germany

Hans Fischer: Nobel Prize for Chemistry 1930 Germany
b. Jul 27, 1881 Hochst, Germany
d. Mar 31, 1945 Munich, Germany

Abe Fortas: US Supreme Court Justice
b. Jun 19, 1910 Memphis TN
d. Apr 5, 1982 Washington DC

John Fox Jr.: Journalist, novelist, short story writer
b. Dec 16, 1862 Stony Point KY
d. Jul 8, 1919 Big Stone Gap VA

Sir Charles Frank: Distinguished British physicist
b. Mar 6, 1911 Durban, South Africa
d. Apr 5, 1998 Bristol, England

Adolph Franosch: German opera singer, bass
b. c1830 Cologne, Germany
d. Aug 6, 1880 NY

Norman Vilsack Frauenheim: Internationally acclaimed
    pianist
b. Oct 29, 1897 Pittsburgh PA
d. Nov 18, 1989 Pittsburgh PA

Dennis Gabor: Nobel Prize for Physics 1971 UK
b. Jun 5, 1900, Budapest, Hungary
d. Feb 8, 1979, London, England

John Galsworthy: English Novelist; Nobel Prize for Litera-
    ture 1932
b. Aug 14, 1867 Kingston Hill, Surrey, England
d. Jan 31, 1933 London, England

Kenny Gardner: Popular tenor with Guy Lombardo
    orchestra
b. Mar 20, 1913 Lakeview IA
d. Jul 26, 2002 Manhasset NY

Herbert Spencer Gasser: Nobel Prize for Physiology/Medi-
    cine 1944 US
b. Jul 5, 1888 Platteville WI
d. May 11, 1963 New York NY

George Gershwin: Composer, songwriter
b. Sep 26, 1898 Brooklyn NY
d. Jul 11, 1937 Los Angeles CA

Ira Gershwin: Lyricist with brother George Gershwin, and
    other composers
b. Dec 6, 1896 New York NY
d. Aug 17, 1983 Beverly Hills CA

Vittorio Giannini: Composer of operas, art songs, symphonies, choral works
b. Oct 19, 1903 Philadelphia PA
d. Nov 28, 1966 New York NY

William Gilbert: Librettist, dramatist, Gilbert and Sullivan
b. Nov 18, 1836 London, England
d. May 29, 1911 Grim's Dyke, Harrow, England

Stephen Girard: Philanthropist, founder of Girard College
b. May 20, 1750 Bordeaux, France
d. Dec 26, 1831 Philadelphia PA

Karl Gjellerup: Nobel Prize for Literature 1917 Denmark
b. Jun 2, 1857 Roholte, Denmark
d. Oct 11/13 1919 Klotzsche, Germany

Mikhail Glinka: Classical Composer
b. Jun 1, 1804 Smolensk, Russia
d. Feb 15, 1857 Berlin, Germany

Christoph Willibald von Gluck: Opera composer
b. Jul 2, 1714 Erasbach, Germany
d. Nov 15, 1787 Vienna, Austria

Hermann Gmeiner: Founder of *SOS Children's Villages* for orphaned children
b. Jun 23, 1919 Vorarlberg, Austria
d. Apr 26, 1986 Innsbruck, Austria

Robert H. Goddard: Early rocket scientist, invented first liquid propelled rocket
b. Oct 5, 1882 Worcester MA
d. Aug 10, 1945 Baltimore MD

Kurt Godel: Mathematician, logician, philosopher
b. Apr 28, 1906 Brno, Austria-Czechoslovakia
d. Jan 14, 1978 Princeton NJ

Alexander Godunov: Russian and American ballet dancer
b. Nov 28, 1949 Sakhalin, Russia
d. May 18, 1995 Hollywood CA

Emilio de Gogorza: Baritone singer, classical and popular
   music concerts
b. May 29, 1874 Brooklyn NY
d. May 10, 1949 New York, New York

Edward Gorey: Cartoonist of the macabre *PBS Mystery Series*
b. Feb 22, 1925 Chicago IL
d. Apr 15, 2000 Hyannis MA

Percy Grainger: Pianist, saxophone player, composer
b. Jul 8, 1882 Melbourne, Australia
d. Feb 20, 1961 White Plains NY

Dobie Gray: Singer, songwriter, soul, country, pop
b. Jul 26, 1940 Simonton TX
d. Dec 6, 2011 Nashville TN

Cecil H. Green: Philanthropist, huge endowments to MIT
   and other colleges
b. Aug 6, 1900 Manchester, England
d. Apr 11, 2003 La Jolla CA

Walter Burley Griffin: Int'l architect; designed Canberra
   (Capitol of Australia)
b. Nov 24, 1876 Maywood IL
d. Feb 11, 1937 Lucknow, India
(See entry for Marion Lucy Mahony Griffin)

Paul Grimm: Artist, desert scenes and Indian portraits
b. Jan 11, 1891 King Williams Town, South Africa
d. Dec 30, 1974 Palm Springs CA

Albert Hackett: Playwright, Pulitzer for *Diary of Anne Frank*;
   Screenwriter, *The Thin Man*, etc.
b. Feb 16, 1900 Nutley NJ
d. Mar 16, 1995 New York City NY
(See entry for wife, Frances Goodrich)

Andrew Smith Hallidie: Mechanical genius, inventor of the
   cable car
b. Mar 16, 1836 London, England
d. Apr 24, 1900 San Francisco CA

Dag Hammarskjold: UN Secretary-General 1953–61; Nobel
Prize for Peace 1961
b. Jul 29, 1905 Jönköping, Sweden
d. Sep 18, 1961 near Ndola, Northern Rhodesia (Zambia)

George Frideric Handel: Composer
b. Feb 23, 1685 Halle, Germany
d. Apr 14, 1759 London, England

Howard Harold Hanson: Composer, conductor, Dir. of *East-man School of Music.*
b. Oct 28, 1896 Wahoo, NE
d. Feb 26, 1981 Rochester NY

Arthur Harden: Nobel Prize for Chemistry 1929 UK
b. Oct 12, 1865 Manchester, England
d. Jun 17, 1940 Bourne End, England

Thomas Hardy: Novelist, short story writer, poet, Far From
the Madding Crowd
b. Jun 2, 1840 Dorchester, England
d. Jan 11, 1928 Dorchester, England

Chandler Harper, Winner of 7 Professional Golf
Tournaments
b. Mar 10, 1914 Portsmouth VA
d. Nov 8, 2004 Portsmouth VA

Odd Hassel: Nobel Prize for Chemistry 1969 Norway
b. May 17, 1897 Oslo, Norway
d. May 15, 1981 Oslo, Norway

Thomas Hastings: Architect: "Carrere and Hastings" (built
NY library)
b. Mar 11, 1860 New York NY
d. Oct 22, 1929 New York NY

Joseph Hayden: Composer "father of the symphony"
b. Mar 31-Apr 1, 1732 Rohrau, Austria
d. May 31, 1809 Vienna, Austria

George "Gabby" Hayes: Actor, vaudeville, Hollywood
  westerns
b. May 7, 1885 Wellsville NY
d. Feb 9, 1969 Burbank CA

Sven Hedin: Explorer, geographer, who mapped central
  Asia
b. Feb 19, 1865 Stockholm, Sweden
d. Nov 26, 1952 Stockholm, Sweden

Verner von Heidenstam: Nobel Prize for Literature 1916
  Sweden
b. Jul 6, 1859 Olshammar, Sweden
d. May 20, 1940 Ovralid, Sweden

Albert Wade Hemsworth: Singer-songwriter, guitarist
b. Oct 1916 Brantford, Ontario, Canada
d. Jan 19, 2002 Montreal, Canada

Milton S. Hershey: Famous candy maker; founder of *Hershey
  Chocolate Company*
b. Sep 13, 1857 Hockersville PA
d. Oct 13, 1945 Hershey PA

Karl Herzfeld: Physicist known for kinetic theory and
  ultrasonics
b. Feb 24, 1892 Vienna, Austria
d. Jun 3, 1978 Washington D. C.

John Richard Hicks: Nobel Prize for Economics 1972 UK
b. Apr 8, 1904 Warwick, England
d. May 20, 1989 London, England

Benny Hill: Comedian
b. Jan 21, 1924 Southampton, England
d. Apr 19, 1992 Teddington, London, England

Paul Hindemith: Composer, conductor
b. Nov 16, 1895 Hanau, Germany
d. Dec 28, 1963 Frankfurt am Main

Sir Cyril Norman Hinshelwood: Nobel Prize for Chemistry
1956 UK
b. Jun 19, 1897 London, England
d. Oct 9, 1967 London, England

Thomas Hobbes: Political philosopher
b. Apr 5, 1588, Westport, Wiltshire, England.
d. Dec 4, 1679 Hardwick Hall, England

Felix Hoffmann: Chemist, inventor of aspirin
b. Jan 21, 1868 Ludwigsburg, Germany
d. Feb 8, 1946 Switzerland

Johns Hopkins: Founder of *Johns Hopkins University and
Hospital*
b. May 19, 1795 Anne Arundel County MD
d. Dec 24, 1873 Baltimore MD

Harry Houdini: Magician, escape artist
b. Mar 24, 1874 Budapest, Hungary
d. Oct 31, 1926 Detroit MI

Sir Godfrey Hounsfield: Nobel Prize for physiology, 1979
UK
b. Aug 28, 1919 Nottinghamshire, England
d. Aug 12, 2004 Kingston upon Thames, England

Edwin Powell Hubble: Astronomer for whom the Hubble
telescope is named
b. Nov 29, 1889 Marshfield, MO
d. Sep 28, 1953 San Marino, CA

David Edward Hughes: invented telegraph printer and
microphone
b. May 16, 1831 London, England
d. Jan 22, 1900 London, England

E.J. Hughes: Artist, painted Canadian landscapes
b. Feb 17, 1913 Vancouver, Canada
d. Jan 5, 2007 Duncan, British Columbia, Canada

Langston Hughes: Afro-American Poet and novelist
b. Feb 1, 1902 Joplin MO
d. May 22, 1967 New York, NY

Cordell Hull: Sec. of State; Founded *United Nations*; Nobel
    Peace Prize 1945
b. Oct 2, 1871 Olympus TN
d. Jul 23, 1955 Washington D. C.

David Hume: Philosopher
b. Apr 26, 1711 Edinburgh, Scotland (old style/Julian
    calendar)
d. Aug 25, 1776 Edinburgh, Scotland

Washington Irving: Author, The Legend of Sleepy Hollow, *Rip
    Van Winkle*
b. Apr 3, 1873 New York NY
d. Nov 28, 1859 Sunnyside NY

Eugene George Istomin: Pianist, protégé of Pablo Casals
b. Nov 26, 1925 New York NY
d. Oct 10, 2003 Washington D. C.

Henry James: Novelist
b. Apr 15, 1843 New York NY
d. Feb 28, 1916 London, England

Robert Joffrey: Dancer, choreographer, founder of *Joffrey
    Ballet Company*
b. Dec 24, 1928? Seattle WA
d. Mar 25, 1988 New York NY

Ben Johnson: Actor in Westerns and other Hollywood
    movies
b. Jun 13, 1918 Osage Indian Res. Foraker OK
d. Apr 8, 1996 Mesa AZ

Crockett Johnson (David Johnson Leisk): Illustrated chil-
    dren's books; Cartoonist *"Barnaby"*
b. Oct 20, 1906 New York NY
d. Jul 11, 1975 Norwalk CT

George Johnson: Lived to be 112
b. May 1, 1894 Philadelphia PA
d. Aug 30, 2006 Richmond CA

Anatol Joukowsky: Dancer, choreographer, folk ballet
b. Aug 18, 1908 Poltava, Ukraine
d. Oct 5, 1998 Menlo Park CA

Augustus Juilliard: Philanthropist, *Juilliard School of Music*
b. Apr 19, 1836 At sea, en route to U.S.
d. Apr 25, 1919 New York NY

Duke Kahanamoku: Olympic swimmer, 3 gold medals, 2
    silver, 1912, 1920, 1924
b. Aug 24, 1890 Honolulu HI
d. Jan 22, 1968 Honolulu HI

Immanuel Kant: Philosopher
b. Apr 22, 1724 Konigsberg, East Prussia
d. Feb 12, 1804 Konigsberg, East Prussia

DeForest Kelley: Actor in *Star Trek*
b. Jan 20, 1920 Atlanta GA
d. Jun 11, 1999 Woodland Hills CA

Frank B. Kellogg: US Sec of State; Nobel Peace Prize 1929
    US
b. Dec 22, 1856 Potsdam, New York
d. Dec 21, 1937 St. Paul, Minnesota

Henry W. Kendall: Nobel prize for physics 1990 US
b. Dec 9, 1926 Boston MA
d. Feb 15, 1999 Wakulla Springs State Park FL

Sir John Cowdery Kendrew: Nobel Prize for Chemistry
    1962 UK
b. Mar 24, 1917 Oxford, England
d. Aug 23 1997 Cambridge, England

Bobby Kerr: Irish-Canadian sprinter, 1908 Olympic Gold
    Medalist

b. Jun 9, 1882 Enniskillen, County Fermanagh, Northern Ireland
d. May 12, 1963 Hamilton, Ontario, Canada

Andre Kertesz: International photographer, pioneered 'distortion techniques
b. Jul 2, 1894 Budapest, Hungary
d. Sept 28, 1985 New York NY

Imre Kertész: Novelist, Nobel Prize for Literature 2002 Hungary
b. Nov 9, 1929 Budapest, Hungary

John Maynard Keynes: Economist
b. Jun 5, 1883 Cambridge, England
d. Apr 21, 1946 Firle, Sussex, England

Soren Kierkegaard: Philosopher
b. May 5, 1813 Copenhagen, Denmark
d. Nov 11, 1855 Copenhagen, Denmark

Sidney Kingsley; Playwright, Pulitzer Prize, *Men in White*
b. Oct 18, 1906 New York NY
d. Mar 20, 1995 Oakland NJ

Ralph Knott: Architect who built the Edwardian Baroque style County Hall, London
b. May 3, 1878 London, England
d. Jan 25, 1929 London, England

Andrei Nikolaevich Kolmogorov: Foremost 20th century Soviet mathematician
b. Apr 25, 1903 Tambov, Russia
d. Oct 20, 1987 Moscow, Russia

Andre Kostelanetz: Classical conductor of international acclaim, pops concerts
b. Dec 22, 1901 St. Petersburg, Russia
d. Jan 13, 1980 Port-au-Prince, Haiti

Otto Krayer: German pharmacology professor who condemned Hitler's policy

b. Oct 22, 1899 Köndringen, Germany
d. Mar 18, 1982 Tucson AZ

Helmet Krebs: Opera tenor
b. Oct 8, 1913 Aachen, Germany
d. Aug 30, 2007 Berlin, Germany

Fritz Kreisler: Violinist, composer
b. Feb 2, 1875 Vienna, Austria
d. Jan 29, 1962 New York NY

Paul R. Krugman: Economist, author, columnist NY Times,
    Nobel prize for economics 2008
b. Feb 28. 1953 Albany NY

Joseph Lagrange: Mathematician and astronomer
b. Jan 25, 1736 Turin, Italy
d. Apr 10, 1813 Paris, France

Dalai Lama (Lhamo Dhondrub): Buddhist leader; Nobel
    Prize for Peace 1989
b. Jul 6, 1935 Taktser, Tibet

Willis Eugene Lamb Jr.: Nobel Prize for Physics 1955 US
b. Jul 12, 1913 Los Angeles CA
d. May 15, 2008 Tucson AZ

Antoni Lange: Poet, novelist, philosopher, translator (15
    languages) of 19th century literature
b. 1861 or 1863 Warsaw, Poland
d. Mar 17, 1929 Warsaw, Poland

Alphonse Laveran: Nobel Prize for Medicine 1907, France
b. Jun 18, 1845 Paris, France
d. May 18, 1922 Paris, France

T.E. Lawrence (Lawrence of Arabia): Adventurer, soldier,
    author, archaeologist
b. Aug 16, 1888 Tremadog, North Wales
d. May 19, 1935 Dorset, England

Gottfried Leibniz: Philosopher (Rationalist), mathematician, co-inventor of calculus
b. Jul 1, 1646 Leipzig, Saxony, Germany
d. Nov 14, 1716 Hanover, Germany

Jay Leno: TV Talk show host
b. Apr 28, 1950 New Rochelle NY

Ruggiero Leoncavallo: Opera composer
b. Mar 8, 1857 Naples, Italy
d. Aug 9, 1919 Tuscany, Italy

C.S. Lewis: Author, children's stories,*The Lion, the Witch and the Wardrobe*
b. Nov 29, 1898 Belfast, Ireland
d. Nov 22, 1963 Oxford, England

Meriwether Lewis: Explorer, "Lewis and Clark"
b. Aug 18, 1774 near Charlottesville VA
d. Oct 11, 1909 near Nashville TN

Gabriel Lippmann: Nobel Prize in Physics 1908 France
b. Aug 16, 1845 Bonnevoie, Luxembourg
d. Jul 13, 1921 at sea (Atlantic)

George Lloyd: Composer, symphonic music, late romantic-classical music
b. Jun 28, 1913 Cornwall, England
d. Jul 3, 1998 London, England

John Locke: Philosopher
b. Aug 29, 1632 Wrington, Somerset, England
d. Oct 28, 1704 Essex, England

Frederick Loewe: Musical theatre composer, *Gigi, My Fair Lady, Camelot, Brigadoon*
b. Jun 10, 1901 Vienna, Austria
d. Feb 14, 1988 Palm Springs CA

Guy Lombardo: Band leader
b. Jun 19, 1902 London, Ontario, Canada
d. Nov 5, 1977 Houston TX

Howard Phillips (H.P.) Lovecraft: Writer of horror fiction
b. Aug 20, 1890 Providence RI
d. Mar 15, 1937 Providence RI

Emanuele Luzzati: Artist, film animator, stage set designer, illustrated children's books
b. Jun 3, 1921 Genoa, Italy
d. Jan 27, 2007 Genoa, Italy

Andre Michel Lwoff: Nobel Prize for Physiology/Medicine
1965 France
b. May 8, 1902 Ainay-le-Château, France
d. Sep 30, 1994 Paris, France

Joaquim Maria Machado de Assis: Novelist, short story
writer, poet
b. Jun 21, 1839 Rio de Janeiro, Brazil
d. Sep 29, 1908 Rio de Janeiro, Brazil

Charles Rennie Mackintosh: Architect and painter
b. Jan 7, 1868 Glasgow, Scotland
d. Dec 10, 1928 London, England

John James Richard Macleod: Nobel Prize for physiology/
medicine (insulin) 1923 UK
b. Sep 6, 1876 Perthshire, Scotland
d. Mar 16, 1935 Aberdeen, Scotland

Maurice Maeterlinck: Nobel Prize for Literature 1911
Belgium
b. Aug 29, 1862 Ghent, Belgium
d. May 6, 1949 Nice, France

Bill Maher: TV host, political satire, *Politically Incorrect*
b. Jan 20, 1956 New York NY

Fritz Mahler: Orchestra conductor
b. Jul 16, 1901 Vienna, Austria
d. Jun 18, 1973 Winston-Salem NC

Bob Maitland: Olympic silver medalist in cycling 1948;
    world champion in 65–69 age category 1989
b. Mar 31, 1924 Birmingham, England
d. Aug 26, 2010 Metz, France

Czeslaw Marek: Composer
b. Sep 16, 1891 Przemysl, Poland
d. Jun 17, 1985 Zurich, Switzerland

John Marston: lead harpist, BBC and London Symphonies,
    and for Sinatra and Beatles
b. Sep 19, 1932 England
d. Feb 4, 2007 London, England

Steve Martin: Comedian
b. Aug 14, 1945 Waco TX

Dr. Benjamin E. Mays: Author, college president, civil rights
    leader, SC Hall of Fame
b. Aug 1, 1894/5 Epworth SC
d. Mar 28, 1984 Atlanta GA

Robert McCormick: Publisher of *Chicago Tribune*
b. Jul 30, 1880 Chicago IL
d. Apr 1, 1955 Wheaton IL

Elijah McCoy: African American inventor with over 50 pat-
    ents, "The real McCoy"
b. May 2, 1843 Colchester, Ontario, Canada
d. Oct 10, 1929 Detroit MI

Henry Louis Mencken: Political correspondent, columnist
b. Sep 12, 1880 Baltimore MD
d. Jan 29, 1956 Baltimore MD

Ismail Merchant: Film producer, director
b. Dec 25, 1936 Bombay, India
d. May 25, 2005 London, England

James A. Michener: Novelist
b. Feb 3, 1907 New York NY
d. Oct 16, 1997 Austin TX

John Stuart Mill: Philosopher, economist
b. May 20, 1806 London, England
d. May 8, 1873 Avignon, France

Cesar Milstein: Nobel Prize for Physiology/Medicine 1984
    Argentina
b. Oct 8, 1927 Bahia Blanca, Argentina
d. Mar 24, 2002 Cambridge MA

Frederic Mistral: Nobel Prize for Literature 1904 France
b. Sep 8, 1830 Maillane, France
d. Mar 25, 1914 Maillane, France

Dimitri Mitropoulos: Orchestra conductor, pianist,
    composer
b. Mar 1, 1896 Athens, Greece
d. Nov 2, 1960 Milan, Italy

Piet Mondrian: Artist — Dutch painter, founder of the neo-
    plastic movement
b. Mar 7, 1872 Amersfoort, Netherlands
d. Feb 1, 1944 New York NY

Carlos Monsivais: Author, journalist, leading intellectual,
    won over 33 awards
b. May 4, 1938 Mexico City, Mexico
d. Jun 19, 2010 Mexico City, Mexico`

Eugenio Montale: Italian poet, Nobel Prize for literature
    1975
b. Oct 12, 1896 Genoa, Italy
d. Sep 12, 1981 Milan, Italy

Stanford Moore: Nobel Prize for Chemistry 1972 US
b. Sep 4, 1913 Chicago IL
d. Aug 23, 1982 New York NY

Henri Mulet: Organist and composer
b. Oct 17, 1878 Paris, France
d. Sep 20, 1967 Draguignan, France

Edvard Munch: Artist, expressionist painter
b. Dec 12, 1863 Loten, Norway
d. Jan 23, 1944 Oslo, Norway

Paul Muni: Actor, Hollywood and Broadway
b. Sep 22, 1895 Lemberg, Galicia, present day: Lviv, Ukraine
d. Aug 25, 1967 Montecito CA

Modest Mussorgsky: Composer
b. Mar 21, 1839 Karevo, Russia
d. Mar 28, 1881 St. Petersburg, Russia

Ralph Nader: Consumer advocate, Public Citizen, presidential candidate, author
b. Feb 27, 1934 Winsted CT

Vidiadhar Surajprasad Naipaul: Novelist, Nobel Prize for Literature 2001, Trinidad
b. Aug 17, 1932 Chaguanas, Trinidad and Tobago

Paul Nash: Artist, painter of war themes and surreal seaside landscapes
b. May 11, 1889 London, England
d. Jul 11, 1946 Boscombe, England

James Nasmyth: Invented steam hammer and other industrial tools
b. Aug 19, 1808 Edinburgh, Scotland
d. May 7, 1890 London, England

Barry Nelson: First actor to play James Bond
b. Apr 16, 1917 San Francisco CA
d. Apr 7, 2007 Bucks County PA

Marcus Nerva: Roman Emperor who enacted humanitarian social reforms
b. Nov 8, 0030 A.D. Narni, Umbria (50 miles from Rome), Italy
d. Jan 27, 0098 Rome, Italy

Sir Isaac Newton: Physicist, mathematician
b. Dec 25, 1642 Woolsthorpe, England (Julian calendar)

d. Mar 20, 1727 London, England
b. Jan 4, 1643 (Gregorian calendar)
d. Mar 31, 1727 (Gregorian calendar)

Friedrich Nietzsche: German philosopher
b. Oct 15, 1844 Saxony, Prussia
d. Aug 25, 1900 Weimar, Germany

Alfred Bernhard Nobel: Established the Nobel Prize for
    peace, literature, etc.
b. Oct 21, 1833 Stockholm, Sweden
d. Dec 10, 1896 San Remo, Italy

Rudolph Nureyev: Ballet star
b. Mar 17, 1938 Irkutsk, Soviet Union
d. Jan 6, 1993 Paris, France

Severo Ochoa: Nobel Prize for Medicine 1959
b. Sep 24, 1905 Luarca, Spain
d. Nov 1, 1993 Madrid, Spain

Buxton Orr: Composer: songs, chamber and orchestral mu-
    sic, films
b. Apr 18, 1924 Glasgow, Scotland
d. Dec 27, 1997 Hereford, England

Douglas Osheroff: Nobel Prize for physics US, 1996
b. Aug 1, 1945 Aberdeen WA

Thomas Paine: Author, *The Rights of Man*
b. Jan 29, 1837 Thetford, England
d. Jun 8, 1809 New York, NY

Blaise Pascal: Mathematician, physicist
b. Jun 19, 1623 Clermont-Ferrand, France
d. Aug 19, 1662 Paris, France

Tony Pastor: Father of vaudeville
b. May 28, 1937 New York NY
d. Aug 26, 1908 Elmhurst NY

Wolfgang Pauli: Physicist, Nobel Prize 1945
b. Apr 25, 1900 Vienna, Austria
d. Dec 15, 1958 Zurich, Switzerland

Guy Pearce: Australian actor
b. Oct 5, 1967 Ely, Cambridgeshire, England

Samuel Pepys: Historian, naval administrator
b. Feb 23, 1633 London, England
d. May 26, 1703 Clapham, England

Charles Peirce: Philosopher, founder of pragmatism
b. Sep 10, 1839 Cambridge MA
d. Apr 19, 1914 Milford PA

Giovanni Battista Pergolesi: Composer of comic opera
b. Jan 4, 1710 Jesi, near Ancona, Italy
d. Mar 16/17, 1736 Pozzuoli, Italy

Claude Piéplu: French actor; activist for nuclear
    disarmament
b. May 9/10, 1923 Paris, France
d. May 24, 2006 Paris, France

Georges Pire a.k.a. Henri Dominique: Nobel Prize for Peace
    1958 Belgium
b. Feb 10, 1910 Dinant, Belgium
d. Jan 30, 1969 Louvain, Belgium

William Pitt: British Prime Minister
b. May 28, 1759 Hayes, England
d. Jan 23, 1806 London, England

Plato: Greek philosopher
b. c428 Athens
d. c348 Athens

Edgar Allan Poe: Short story writer; poet
b. Jan 19, 1809 Boston MA
d. Oct 7, 1849 Baltimore MD

James K. Polk: President of the United States •
b. Nov 2, 1795 Mecklenburg NC
d. Jun 15, 1849 Nashville TN

Alexander Pope: Poet, translator of Homer
b. May 21, 1688 London, England
d. May 30, 1744 Twickenham, England

Cole Porter: Song writer
b. Jun 9, 1891 Peru IN
d. Oct 15, 1964 Santa Monica, CA

Attilio Poto: Clarinetist, conductor: *Metropolitan Opera Company, Boston Symphony*
b. 1915 Boston MA
d. Jul 24, 2003 Boston MA

Edward Henry Potthast: American Impressionist artist
b. Jun 10, 1857 Cincinnati OH
d. Mar 9, 1927 New York NY

Nicolas Poussin: French-Italian painter
b. Jun 15, 1594 Normandy, France
d. Nov 19, 1665 Rome, Italy

Fritz Pregl: Nobel Prize in Chemistry 1923 Austria
b. Sep 3, 1869 Ljubljana, Austria-Hungary (now Slovenia)
d. Dec 13, 1930 Graz, Austria

Jack Prelutsky: Author of children's poems, "children's poet laureate"
b. Sep 8, 1940 Brooklyn NY

Sully Prudhomme: Poet, first Nobel Prize for Literature 1901 France
b. Mar 16, 1839 Paris, France
d. Sep 6, 1907 Chatenay-Malabry, France

Qigong a.k.a. Qi Gong: Renowned calligrapher, artist, painter
b. Jul 26, 1912 Beijing, China
d. Jun 30, 2005 Beijing, China

Argeo Quadri: Opera conductor
b. Mar 23, 1911 Como, Italy
d. Apr 14, 2004 Milan, Italy

Maurice Ravel: Composer *Bolero*
b. Mar 7, 1875 Ciboure, France
d. Dec 28, 1937 Paris, France

Wilson Rawls: Novelist
b. Sep 24, 1913 Scraper OK
d. Dec 16, 1984 Idaho Falls ID

Man Ray: Artist, Dada and Surrealism
b. Aug 27, 1890 Philadelphia PA
d. Nov 18, 1976 Paris, France

Martin Rees: Astrophysicist, author
b. Jun 23, 1942 Shropshire, England

Travis Reeves: Country singer
b. Aug 20, 1923 Galloway TX
d. Jul 31, 1964 near Nashville TN

Ottorino Respighi: Classical composer
b. Jul 9, 1879 Bologna, Italy
d. Apr 18, 1936 Rome, Italy

Wladyslaw Stanislaw Reymont: Nobel Prize for Literature
    1924 Poland
b. May 7, 1867 Radomsko, Poland
d. Dec 5, 1925 Warsaw, Poland

Sir Joshua Reynolds: Painter
b. 1723 Plympton, England
d. 1792 London, England

Robert L. Ripley: *Ripley's Believe it or Not*
b. Dec 25, 1890 Santa Rosa CA
d. May 27, 1949 New York NY

James Rizzi Pop artist, official artist for 1996 summer
Olympics
b. Oct 5, 1950 Brooklyn NY
d. Dec 24, 1911 New York NY

Jerome Robbins: Choreographer: *American Ballet Theatre, NYC Ballet*, Broadway
b. Oct 11, 1918 New York NY
d. Jul 29, 1998 New York NY

Isaac Roberts: Astronomer: awarded Gold Medal of the
Royal Astronomical Society
b. Jan 27, 1829 Y Groes, Wales
d. Jul 17, 1904 Starfield, Crowboro, Sussex, England

William Barton Rogers: Founder of *Massachusetts Institute of Technology*
b. Dec 7, 1804 Philadelphia PA
d. May 30, 1882 Cambridge MA

Romain Rolland: Nobel Prize for Literature 1915 France
b. Jan 29, 1866 Clamecy, France
d. Dec 30, 1944 Vezelay, France

Sigmund Romberg: Composer of operettas, *Desert Song, Student Prince*
b. Jul 29, 1887 Gross-Kanizsa , Hungarian
d. Nov 9, 1951 New York NY

Gioacchino Rossini: Composer, *William Tell Overture*
b. Feb 29, 1792 Pesaro, Italy
d. Nov 13, 1868 Passy (near Paris), France

Sir Joseph Rotblat: Nobel Peace Prize, 1995 UK
b. Nov 4, 1908 Warsaw Poland
d. Aug 31, 2005 London, England

Theodore Rousseau: Artist from the Barbizon school of
landscape painters
b. Apr 15, 1812 Paris, France
d. Dec 22, 1867 Barbizon, France

Louis Rubenstein, North America's first world figure-skating champion.
b. Sep 23, 1861 Montreal, Canada
d. Jan 3, 1931 Montreal, Canada

Leopold Ruzicka: Nobel Prize for chemistry, 1939
b. Sep 3, 1887 Vukovar, Croatia
d. Sep 26, 1976 Zurich, Switzerland

Manuel Salazar: Opera tenor
b. Jan 3, 1887 San Jose, Costa Rica
d. Aug 6, 1950 San Jose, Costa Rica

George Santayana: Philosopher, poet, novelist
b. Dec 16, 1863 Madrid, Spain
d. Sep 26, 1952 Rome, Italy

Jean-Paul Sartre: Philosopher
b. Jun 21, 1905 Paris, France
d. Apr 15, 1980 Paris, France

Erik Satie: Composer
b. May 17, 1866 Honfleur, Normandy, France
d. Jul 1, 1925 Paris, France

Will Schaefer: Composer of TV music; won Pulitzer Prize
b. Nov 23, 1928 Kenosha WI
d. Jun 30, 2007 Cathedral CA

Max Schmeling: World heavyweight boxing champion
b. Sep 28, 1905 Klein Luckow, Germany
d. Feb 2, 2005 Wenzendorf, Germany

Otto H. Schmitt: Biophysicist, "inventor extraordinaire" invented Schmitt trigger circuit
b. Apr 6, 1913 St. Louis MO
d. Jan 6, 1998 Minneapolis MN

Franz Schubert: Composer
b. Jan 31, 1797 Vienna
d. Nov 19, 1828 Vienna

Julian Schwinger: Nobel Prize for Physics 1965 US
b. Feb 12, 1918 New York NY
d. Jul 16, 1994 Los Angeles CA

Maurice Sendak: Author and illustrator of children's books
b. Jun 10, 1928 Brooklyn NY
d. May 8, 2012 Danbury CT

George Bernard Shaw: Playwright, lecturer, Nobel Prize for
    Literature 1925
b. Jul 26, 1856 Dublin, Ireland
d. Nov 2, 1950 Ayot St. Lawrence, England

Ted Shawn: Modern ballet dancer and choreographer; Den-
    ishawn dancers
b. Oct 21, 1891 Kansas City MO
d. Jan 9, 1972 Orlando FL

James Sherard: Noted botanist, apothecarist
b. Nov 1, 1666 Leicestershire, England
d. Feb 12, 1738 Leicestershire, England

Zachary Solov: Ballet dancer; choreographer for the *Metro-
    politan Opera*
b. Feb 15, 1923 Philadelphia PA
d. Nov 6, 2004 New York NY

Baruch Spinoza: Philosopher, rationalist (reason as basis for
    knowledge)
b. Nov 24, 1632 Amsterdam, Netherlands
d. Feb 21, 1677 Hague, Netherlands

Henry Spira: Founded Animal Rights Int'l; got Revlon to
    stop using animal testing
b. Jun 19, 1927 Antwerp, Belgium
d. Sep 12, 1998 New York NY

Freelan Oscar Stanley: Inventor of the steam-powered
    automobile
b. Jun 1, 1849 Kingfield ME
d. Oct 2, 1940 Kingfield ME

Hermann Staudinger: Nobel Prize for Chemistry 1953 West
   Germany
b. Mar 23, 1881 Worms, Hesse, German Empire
d. Sep 8, 1965 Freiburg, Germany

Prof. Ian Stevenson: Author, authority on the study of reincarnation; Univ. of VA
b. Oct 31, 1918 Montreal, Canada
d. Feb 8, 2007 Charlottesville VA

Johann Strauss Jr.: Composer, the "Waltz King"
b. Oct 25, 1825 Vienna, Austria
d. Jun 3, 1899 Vienna, Austria

Thomas Sigismund Stribling, Novelist, Pulitzer Prize
   1933, *The Store*
b. Mar 4, 1881 Clifton TN
d. Jul 8, 1965 Florence AL

Rodney Strong: Broadway dancer and American winemaker
b. 1927 Camus WA
d. Mar 5, 2006 Healdsburg CA

Otto Struve: Astronomer, proved ionized hydrogen in the
   interstellar medium
b. Aug 12, 1897 Kharkov, Ukraine
d. Apr 6, 1963 Berkeley CA

Arthur Sullivan: Composer (Gilbert & Sullivan)
b. May 13, 1842 London, England
d. Nov 22, 1900 London, England

Shinichi Suzuki: Violinist, taught thousands of young children to play violin, "Suzuki method"
b. Oct 17, 1898 Nagoya, Japan
d. Jan 26, 1998 Matsumoto, Japan

Emanuel Swedenborg: Philosopher, Mystic
b. Jan 29, 1688 Stockholm, Sweden
d. Mar 29, 1772 London, England

Jean Tabaud: Portrait artist; ballet dancer

b. Jul 5, 1914 Saujon, France
d. Dec 2, 1996 Pawling NY

Edgar A. Tafel: Award winning architect, designed church-
es, college campuses
b. Mar 12, 1912 New York NY
d. Jan 18, 2011 New York NY

Thomas Tallis: Composer, organist
b. c1505 Leicestershire, England
d. Nov 25, 1585 Greenwich, England

Chris R. Tame: Founder and president of Libertarian
Alliance
b. Dec 20, 1949 Enfield, England
d. Mar 20, 2006 London, England

Pyotr Tchaikovsky: Composer
b. May 7, 1840 Votkinsk, Russia
d. Nov 6, 1893 St. Petersburg, Russia

Nikola Tesla: Inventor of radio, electric alternating current
b. Jul 9/10, 1856 (b. midnight) Smiljan, Croatia
d. Jan 7, 1943 New York NY

Glen Tetley: Dancer-choreographer, modern and classical
ballet; Joffrey Ballet Co.
b. Feb 3. 1926 Cleveland OH
d. Jan 26, 2007 West Palm Beach FL

Thales: Greek Philosopher
b. 624 BC Miletus
d. 546 BC Miletus

Ernest Lawrence Thayer: Wrote famous poem: *Casey at the
Bat*
b. Aug 14, 1863 Lawrence MA
d. Aug 21, 1940 Santa Barbara CA

Hank Thompson: Country singing star
b. Sept 3, 1925 Waco TX
d. Nov 6, 2007 Keller TX

Ralph Thompson: Artist of animal paintings and drawings,
  book illustrator
b. Jun 3, 1913 Thorner, West Yorkshire, England
d. May 3, 1909 Cookham Dean, Berkshire, England

William Thompson: Political philosopher, social reformer,
  egalitarian and utilitarian
b. 1775 Cork, Ireland
d. Mar 28, 1833 Cork, Ireland

Virgil Thomson: Composer, American sound in classical
  music
b. Nov 25, 1896 Kansas City MO
d. Sep 30, 1989 New York NY

Henry David Thoreau: Philosopher, author, *Walden*
b. Jul 12, 1817 Concord MA
d. May 6, 1862 Concord MA

Alexis de Tocqueville: Political philosopher and historian,
  Democracy in America
b. Jul 29, 1805 Paris, France
d. Apr 16, 1859 Cannes, France

Emiliano Mercado del Toro: lived to be 115
b. Aug 21, 1891 Puerto Rico
d. Jan 24, 2007 Isabela, Puerto Rico

Raffaele Tudisco: Founder, *Amici Opera Co.*, first to perform
  in all 26 Verdi operas
b. 1958 Mt. Airy, Philadelphia PA

William Tutte: Mathematician and cryptographer, cracked
  German code WWII
b. May 14, 1917 Newmarket, Suffolk, England
d. May 2, 2002 Waterloo, Ontario, Canada

Deon Van der Walt: International opera tenor
b. Jul 28, 1958 Cape Town, South Africa
d. Nov 29, 2005 Paarl, South Africa

Luther Vandross: Grammy winning popular rhythm and
blues singer
b. Apr 20, 1951 New York NY
d. Jul 1, 2005 Edison NJ

Johann Baptist Vanhal (a.k.a. Wanhal): Classical composer
b. May 12, 1739 Nechanice, Bohemia
d. Aug 20, 1813 Vienna, Austria

Richard Verderber: Fencing, silver medal, 1912 Olympics;
national championships, sabre and foil fencing
b. Jan 23, 1884 Kocevje, Slovenia
d. Sep 8, 1955 Vienna, Austria

Amerigo Vespucci: Explorer and cartographer for whom
America is named
b. Mar 9, 1454 Florence, present day Italy
d. Feb 22, 1512, Seville, present day Spain

William Vickrey: Nobel Prize for economics 1996, US
b. Jun 21, 1914 Victoria British Columbia, Canada
d. Oct 11, 1996 Harrison NY

Heitor Villa-Lobos: Composer, symphonies, operas, ballets,
choral music
b. Mar 5, 1887 Rio de Janeiro, Brazil
d. Nov 17, 1959 Rio de Janeiro, Brazil

Antonio Vivaldi: Composer
b. Mar 4, 1678 Venice, Italy
d. Jul 28, 1738 Vienna, Austria

Stanley "Stan" Wagner: Olympic gold medal, ice hockey 1932
b. Mar 2, 1908 Pueblo CO
d. Oct 11, 2002 in Winnipeg, Canada

Christopher Walken: Actor
b. Mar 31, 1943 New York NY

Otto Wallach: Nobel Prize for Chemistry 1910 Germany
b. Mar 27, 1847 Königsberg, Germany
d. Feb 26, 1931 Gottingen, Germany

William Walton: Composer, chamber, concerto and vocal
     music
b. Mar 29, 1902 Oldham, Lancashire, England
d. Mar 8, 1983 Ischia, Italy

Felix Wankel: Invented the rotary engine; animal rights
     advocate
b. Aug 13, 1902 Lahr, Germany
d. Oct 9, 1988 Lindau, Germany

Otto Warburg, Nobel Prize for physiology/Medicine 1931
     Germany
b. Oct 8, 1883 Freiburg, Germany
d. Aug 1, 1970 Berlin, Germany

Andy Warhol: Pop artist icon
b. Aug 6, 1928 Pittsburgh PA
d. Feb 22, 1987 New York NY

Leonard Warren: Baritone, *Metropolitan Opera*
b. Apr 21, 1911 New York city NY
d. Mar 4, 1960 New York City NY

Dale Wasserman: Playwright: *Man of La Mancha*
b. Nov 2, 1914 Rhinelander WI
d. Dec 21, 2008 Paradise Valley AZ

Bill Watterson: Cartoonist, *Calvin and Hobbes*
b. Jul 5, 1958 Washington D. C.

Roy Webb: Film composer for *RKO Pictures*
b. Oct 3, 1888 New York NY
d. Dec 10, 1982 Santa Monica CA

H.T. Webster: Political cartoonist, *The Timid Soul*, character
     Caspar Milquetoast
b. 1885 Parkersburg WV
d. Sep 22, 1952 on way home to Stamford CT

Kurt Weill: Composer, Musical theatre, orchestral works,
     Three Penny Opera

b. Mar 2, 1900 Dessau, Germany
d. Apr 3, 1950 New York NY

Patrick White: Novelist, Nobel Prize for Literature 1973
  Australia
b. May 28, 1912 London, England
d. Sep 30, 1990 Sydney, Australia

Bernie Whitebear: Native American leader; founder of
  United Indians of All Tribes Foundation
b. Sep 27, 1937 Nespelem, Washington
d. Jul 16, 2000 Seattle WA

Walt Whitman, Poet
b. May 31, 1819 West Hills NY
d. Mar 26, 1892 Camden NJ

George Wightwick: Prominent English architect and archi-
  tectural journalist
b. 26 August 1802 near Mold, Flintshire, Wales
d. July 9, 1872 Portishead, England

Thornton Wilder: American playwright, Pulitzer Prize
b. Apr 17, 1897 Madison, WI
d. Dec 7, 1975 Hamden CT

Ralph Vaughan Williams: Composer, chamber, choral, opera, orchestra, symphony
b. Oct 12, 1872 Down Ampney, England
d. Aug 26, 1958 London, England

Tennessee Williams: Playwright, Pulitzer Prize for *Street
  Car Named Desire*
b. Mar 26, 1911 Columbus MS
d. Feb 25, 1983 New York NY

Eli Marsden Wilson: Artist, etcher, engraver, painter (m. to
  artist Hilda Mary Pemberton)
b. Jun 24, 1877 Ossett, Yorkshire, England
d. Nov 13, 1965 London, England

Kenneth G. Wilson: Nobel prize for Physics 1982 US
b. Jun 8, 1936 Waltham MA

Ludwig Wittgenstein: Philosopher, *Tractatus
Logico-Philosophicus*
b. Apr 26, 1889 Vienna, Austria
d. Apr 29, 1951 Cambridge, England

Orville Wright: Aviator
b. Aug 19, 1871 Dayton OH
d. Jan 30, 1948 Dayton OH

Wilbur Wright: Aviator
b. Apr 16, 1867 Midville IN
d. May 30, 1912 Dayton OH

Liu Xiaobo: Nobel Peace Prize 2010
b. Dec 28, 1955 Changchun, Jilin, China

Franciszek Zachara: Pianist, composer
b. Dec 10, 1898 Tarnow, Poland
d. Feb 2, 1966 Tallahassee, Florida

Emil Zatopek; Olympic gold medals runner, broke 18 world
records
b. Sep 19, 1922 Koprivnice, Czechoslovakia
d. Nov 22, 2000 Prague, Czechoslovakia

Alberto Zelman: Violinist and conductor
b. Nov 15, 1874 Melbourne, Australia
d. Mar 3, 1927 Melbourne, Australia

Bibliography

Books

Alvera, Pierluigi: *Respighi*; Treves Publishing Company 1986
Subject: Respighi, Ottorino

Anawalt, Sasha: *Joffrey Ballet — Robert Joffrey and the Making of an American Dance Company*, Scribner NY 1996
Subject: Robert Joffrey

Conrad, Christine: *Jerome Robbins That Broadway Man That Ballet Man*, Booth-Clibborn 2000 London, p.12 "When I met him in 1965, he felt time was running out if he was ever to marry and have children."
Subject: Jerome Robbins

Cruz, Barbara C.: *Alvin Ailey Celebrating African-American Culture in Dance*, Enslow Publishers NJ 2004
Subject: Alvin Ailey

Gill, Brendan: *Late Bloomers*, Artisan NY 1996 p.80 "Hamilton's father was a rich American from the Middle West, who appears to have devoted his life to the rearing and

domination of his children — none of them married until after his death and none had children."
Subjects: Alice and Edith Hamilton

Ilupina, Anna: *Galina Ulanova: Ballerina The Life and Work of Galina Ulanova*, Provident Publishing Co., Philadelphia 1965
Subject: Galina Ulanova

Kroeger, Brook: *Nellie Bly*, Timber Books, Random House c1994 p.298 "Like Bly, neither of her brothers had children."
Subject: Nellie Bly

Johnson, Paul: *Creators*, HarperCollins Publishers 2006 NY
Subjects:
Jane Austen p.119
T.S. Eliot p.207

McGrayne, Sharon Bertsch: *Nobel Prize Women in Science*, A Birch Lane Press Book, Carol Pub. Group NY 1993, pp.37–63
Subject: Lise Meitner

Nass Esq., Herbert E.: *Wills of the Rich and Famous*, Gramercy Books NY 1991 & 2000;
Subjects:
May West, p.57, "I declare . . . and that I have no children, living or dead. "
Kate Smith, p.203 "She never married and had no children." and "I have never married during my lifetime. My sister and nieces are my sole blood relatives . . ."
Rudolph Nureyev, p.285 "During his lifetime, Nureyev never married and had no children."
Lillian Hellman, p.374 "At the time of her death, Ms. Hellman was not married and had no children."
James Beard, p.380 "I declare that I am not married and have no children."

O'Neill, John J.: *Prodigal Genius The Life of Nikola Tesla*; Adventures Unlimited Press, USA 2008, p.6
Subject: Nikola Tesla

Paine, Thomas: *Rights of Man*, Easton Press collector's ed. Norwalk CT 1979: From Introduction, p.v
Subject: Thomas Paine

Poe, Edgar Allan: *Tales of Mystery and Imagination*; Easton Press Westport CT 1975; introduction p.xiv
Subject: Edgar Allan Poe

Strobel, Heinrich: *Paul Hindemith*, B. Schott's Sohne, Mainz, Germany 1961
Photo biography of Hindemith and wife but no photos or mention of children
Subject: Paul Hindemith

Terry, Walter: *Great Male Dancers of the Ballet*, Anchor Books (Anchor Press/Double Day) NY 1978

Rasponi, Lanfranco: *The Last Prima Donnas*, Alfred A. Knopf, NY 1982, p.55
Subject: Dame Eva Turner

Schraff, Anne: *Harriet Tubman Moses of the Underground Railroad*; Enslow Publishers Inc. Berkeley Heights NJ 2001
Subject: Harriet Tubman

Trobridge, George: *Swedenborg Life and Teaching*, Swedenborg Foundation Inc. NY 1962 (published by Rand McNally & Co, p.31) Provides information regarding his broken engagement to a young girl who was to be his wife, as arranged by the girl's father, and Swedenborg's solemn oath to never again consider marriage.
Subject: Emanuel Swedenborg

Wheaton, Elizabeth: *Ms.: The Story of Gloria Steinem*, Morgan Reynolds Publishers Inc.; Greensboro NC 2002
Subject: Gloria Steinem

Biographical Collections

Schlessinger, Bernard S. and June H.: *The Who's Who of Nobel Prize Winners* 1901–1990 2nd ed. , Oryx Press, Phoenix AZ 1991:

For some Nobel laureates, the Schlessingers state, "Children: No record found. " The following Nobel laureates they list as having no children:

Nobel winners for chemistry (1901–1990):
Otto Wallach 1910; Francis William Aston 1922; Fritz Pregl 1923; Sir Arthur Harden 1929; Hans Fischer 1930; Leopold Stephen Ruzicka 1939; Hermann Staudinger 1953; Sir Cyril Norman Hinshelwood 1956; Sir John Cowdery Kendrew 1962; Odd Hassel 1969; Stanford Moore 1972; Ernest Otto Fischer 1973; Donald James Cram 1987
Nobel winners for economics (1969–1990 — this award was first issued in 1969):
John Richard Hicks 1972; James McGill Buchanan 1986

Nobel winners for literature (1901–1990):
Sully Prudhomme 1901; Frederic Mistral 1904; Selma Lagerlof 1909; Maurice Maeterlinck 1911; Romain Rolland 1915; Verner von Heidenstam 1916; Karl Gjellerup 1917; Jacinto Benavente 1922; Wladyslaw Stanislaw Reymont 1924; George Bernard Shaw 1925; John Galsworthy 1932; Thomas Stearns Eliot 1948; Par Fabian Lagerkvist 1951; Halldor Kiljan Laxness 1955; Juan Ramon Jimenez 1956; Saint John Perse 1960; Ivo Andric 1961; Giorgos Seferis 1963; Jean Paul Sartre 1964; Nelly Sachs 1966; Samuel Beckett 1969; Patrick White 1973; Harry Edmund Martinson 1974; Eugenio Montale 1975; Vincent Aleixandre 1977; Elytis Odysseus 1979
Note: Par Fabian Lagerkvist, 1951 for Literature had two sons according to the online biography NNDB: http://www.nndb. com/people/222/000087958/

Nobel winners for Medicine/Physiology (1901–1990)
Elie Metchnikoff 1908; Alexis Carrel 1912; John James Richard MacLeod 1923; Johannes Fibiger 1926; Otto Warburg 1931; Henrik Peter Dam 1943; Herbert Spencer Gasser 1944; Antonio Egas Moniz 1949; Severo Ochoa 1959; George von Bekesy 1961; Andre Michael Lwoff 1965; Marshall Warren Nirenberg 1968; Sir Godfrey Hounsfield 1979; Barbara McClintock 1983; Cesar Milstein 1984; Joseph Leonard Goldstein 1985; Rita Levi-Montalcini 1986; Gertrude Bell Elion 1988

Nobel winners for Peace (1901–1990)
Jean Henri Dunant 1901; Charles Albert Gobat 1902; Sir
William Randal Cremer 1903; Bertha von Süttner 1905;
Auguste Beernaert 1909; Aristide Briand 1926; Ludwig
Quidde 1927; Frank Billings Kellogg 1929; Laura Jane
Addams 1931; Sir Norman Angell 1933; Edgar Robert
Cecil 1937; Cordell Hull 1945; Emily Greene Balch 1946;
Leon Jouhaux 1951; George Catlett Marshall 1953; Rev.
Dominique Pire 1958; Dag Hammarskjold 1961; Rene
Cassin 1968; Mairead Corrigan/Peace People 1976;
Mother Teresa 1979; Dalai Lama 1989

Nobel winners for Physics (1901–1990)
Gabriel Lippmann 1908; Louis-Victor Broglie 1929; Erwin
Schrodinger 1933; Victor Franz Hess 1936; Otto Stern
1943; Wolfgang Pauli 1945; Willis Eugene Lamb Jr. 1955;
Johannes Hans Jensen 1963; Julian Schwinger 1965; Dennis Gabor 1971; John Hasbrouck van Vleck 1977; Kenneth Geddes Wilson 1982; Sub Chandrasekhar

Reference Books

These reference materials are used as supplemental sources
only. Most of these reference works list spouses' names with year
of marriage; and list "s" for son and "d" for daughter: e.g., one s; one
d. ; or e.g., 1s, 1d. *Who's Who in America*, Marquis, Chicago IL; since
1898, lists "children." The names below show no listings of children.

International Who Was Who; Europa Publications Ltd. London, England

International Who's Who in Classical Music, Europa Publications Ltd. London, England

International Who's Who in Music and Musicians' Directory, Edited by Ernest
Kay, Melrose Press Ltd. , Cambridge, England, 7th edition 1975;
10th ed. 1985; 12th ed. 1990/91 edited by David M. Cummings and
Dennis K. McIntire

Who Was Who in America, Marquis Who's Who Inc. Chicago IL

Who Was Who in America With World Notables; Marquis, New Providence
NJ

Who's Who, St. Martin's Press NY until 2000; then 2000–4 A & C Black Pub Inc. NY; 2005- "Bloomsbury" A & C Black Pub Inc NY; volume numbering is a continuation of St. Martin's volume numbers.

Alda, Frances: *Who's Who in America*, vol.25, 1948–49, p. 38

Anderson, Marion: *Who's Who in America*, vol.36, 1970–71, p. 46

Bampton, Rose E.: *International Who's Who in Music and Musicians' Directory*, 12th ed. p. 40

Barber, Samuel: *Who Was Who in America* vol.7, 1977–81 p. 29; *International Who's Who in Music and Musicians' Directory*, 1975 ed. p. 49

Beebe, William: *Who Was Who*, Adams & Black, London, 1961–70 p. 79

Begg, Heather: *International Who's Who in Classical Music*, vol. 2004 p. 63

Bergé, Irénée Marius: *Who Was Who in America*, vol.1, 1897–1942, p. 87

Blackwell, Alice Stone *Who Was Who in America*, vol.2, 1943–50, p. 13

Britten, Benjamin: *International Who's Who in Music and Musicians' Directory*, 1975 ed. p. 115

Blitzstein, Marc : *International Who's Who in Music and Musicians' Directory*, 1975 ed. p. 91

Brown, Helen Gurley: *Who's Who in America*, 2006, 60th ed. vol.1, p. 577

Bruhn, Erik: *Who's Who*, 1985–86 p. 253; International Who's Who, 50th ed. , 1986–87, p. 217

Cage, John: *International Who's Who in Music and Musicians' Directory*, 1975 ed. p. 140

Carver, George Washington, *Who Was Who in America*, 1950 vol.2 p. 106

Copland, Aaron: *International Who's Who in Music and Musicians' Directory*, 1975 ed. p. 184

Corelli, Franco: *International Who's Who in Music and Musicians' Directory*, 1990/91 ed. p. 158

Crespin, Regine: *International Who's Who in Classical Music*, vol. 2004 p. 179

Cruz, Celia: *International Who's Who*, 63 ed. , 2000, p. 348

Cukor, George: *Who Was Who in America*, vol.VIII,1982–85, p. 94; *Who's Who in America* 42nd ed. 1982–3, vol.1, p. 722

Farrell, Suzanne: *Who's Who in America*, 2006, 60th ed. p. 1414

Hanson, Howard: *International Who's Who in Music and Musicians' Directory*, 1975 ed. p. 368

Istomin, Eugene George: *International Who's Who in Music and Musicians' Directory*, 1990/91 ed. p. 411

Koner, Pauline: *Who's Who in America*, 2001 55th ed. p. 2912

Kostelanetz, Andre: *International Who's Who in Music and Musicians' Directory*, 1975 ed. p. 498

Krebs, Helmut, *International Who's Who in Classical Music*, vol. 2004 p. 476

Kreisler, Fritz: *Who Was Who in America*, vol.IV, (1961–68) p. 543

Leigh, Adele: *International Who's Who in Classical Music*, vol. 2004 p. 509

Lenya, Lotte: *Who's Who in America*, vol.vol.35, 1970–71, p. 1343

Lloyd, George: *International Who's Who in Music and Musicians' Directory*, 1985 ed. p. 546

Mahler, Fritz: *Who Was Who in America*, vol.VI p. 2601; *International Who's Who in Music and Musicians' Directory*, 1975 ed. p. 579

McCoy, Elijah: *Who Was Who in America*, vol.IV (1961–68) p. 632

Newlin, Dika: *International Who's Who in Classical Music*, vol. 2004 p. 623

Nielson, Inga: *International Who's Who in Classical Music*, vol. 2004 p. 625

Nilsson (a.k.a. Nilson), Birgit: *International Who's Who in Music and Musicians' Directory*, 12th ed. p. 631

Orr, Buxton: *International Who's Who in Music and Musicians' Directory*, 1985 ed. p. 671

Page, Ruth: *Who's Who in America*, 45th ed. 1988–9 p. 2369; *Who's Who in America* 1964–5 p. 1535

Pons, Lily: *Who's Who in America*, vol.33 1964–65 p. 1602; Who's Who 1970–1 p. 2482

Ponselle, Rosa: *Who's Who in America*, vol.25 1948–49 p. 1974

Price, Leontyne: *Who's Who in America*, vol.33, 1964–65 p. 1619; *Who's Who* 1985–86 p. 1558; International *Who's Who in Classical Music*, vol. 2004 p. 700

Rankin, Nell: *International Who's Who in Classical Music*, vol. 2004 p. 714

Ripley, Robert L.: *Who Was Who in America*, vol.2, 1943–1950 p. 450

Schwarzkopf, Dame Elizabeth: *International Who's Who in Classical Music*, vol. 2004 p. 785

Shawn, Ted: *Who's Who in America*, vol.36 1970–71 m. Ruth St. Denis

Strickland, Lily: *Who's Who in America*, vol.25, 1948–49, p. 2400

Suzuki, Shinichi: *International Who's Who in Music and Musicians' Directory*, 1975 ed. p. p. 883

Tebaldi, Renata: *International Who's Who in Classical Music*, vol. 2004 p. 862

Tetley, Glen: *Who's Who*, 2007 p. 2242; *Who's Who in America*, 1985–6, p. 1901

Thomson, Virgil: *International Who's Who in Music and Musicians' Directory*, 1985 ed. p. 898

Tourel, Jennie: *Who's Who in America*, vol.36, 1970–71, p. 2294

Turner, Dame Eva/Edith: *Who's Who*, 1985–86 p. 1953; *International Who's Who in Music and Musicians' Directory*, 1975 ed. p. 922

Uchida, Mitsuko: *International Who's Who in Classical Music*, vol. 2004 p. 888

Ulanova, Galina: *Who's Who*, St. Martins 1985–6 p. 1961

Van der Walt, Deon: *International Who's Who in Music and Musicians' Directory*, 1990/91 ed. p. 875 (listed under Walt)

Varnay, Astrid: *International Who's Who in Classical Music*, vol. 2004 p. 897

Vaness, Carol: *International Who's Who in Music and Musicians' Directory*, 12ed. p. 860

Votipka, Thelma: *Who's Who in America*, vol.33, 1964–65, p. 2075

Walton, Sir William: *International Who's Who in Music and Musicians' Directory*, 1975 ed. p. 960

Online Resources

The author of this work has carefully researched the 700 names herein, including some 1400 web site references. The author's most frequently used web references include:

Encyclopedia.com. http://www.encyclopedia.com/

The Guardian. http://www.guardian.co.uk

Los Angeles Times. www.latimes.com

The New York Times. NYTimes.com.

NNDB. http://www.nndb.com/

Profiles of Great Composers; formerly *Profiles of Great Classical Composers.* http://www.52composers.com/index.html

The Telegraph Online. http://www.telegraph.co.uk

Wikipedia. http://www.wikipedia.org/

Women in World History: A Biographical Encyclopedia. http://www.encyclopedia.com/Women+in+World+History-C-+A+Biographical+ Encyclopedia/publications.aspx?pageNumber=1